Contents

Homeless Children

of related interest

Social Work with Children and Families
Getting into Practice
Ian Butler and Gwenda Roberts
ISBN 1 85302 365 5

Child Welfare Services
Developments in Law, Policy, Practice and Research
Edited by Malcolm Hill and Jane Aldgate
ISBN 1 85302 316 7

Housing and Social Exclusion
Edited by Fiona E. Spiers
ISBN 1 85302 638 7

Social Care and Housing
Edited by Ian Shaw, Susan Lambert and David Clapham
ISBN 1 85302 437 6

Effective Ways of Working with Children and their Families
Edited by Malcolm Hill
ISBN 1 85302 619 0
Research Highlights in Social Work 35

Troubles of Children and Adolescents
Edited by Ved Varma
ISBN 1 85302 323 X

Working with Children in Need
Studies in Complexity and Challenge
Edited by Eric Sainsbury
ISBN 1 85302 275 6

Homeless Children

Problems and Needs

Edited by Panos Vostanis and Stuart Cumella

Jessica Kingsley Publishers
London and Philadelphia

First published in the United Kingdom in 1999 by
Jessica Kingsley Publishers Ltd, 116 Pentonville Road
London N1 9JB, England
and
325 Chestnut Street, Philadelphia, PA 19106, U S A
www.jkp.com

Copyright © 1999 Jessica Kingsley Publishers

Library of Congress Cataloging in Publication Data
A CIP catalog record for this book is available from the Library of Congress

British Library Cataloguing in Publication Data
Homeless children : problems and needs
1.Homeless children - Great Britain
I.Vostanis, Panos II.Cumella, Stuart
362.7'08691'0941

ISBN 1 85302 595 X

Printed and Bound in Great Britain by
Athenaeum Press, Gateshead, Tyne and Wear

CHAPTER 1

Introduction

Stuart Cumella and Panos Vostanis

Around the world, the homeless are numbered in tens of millions. Families are born, live and die on the streets of the vast cities of the third world. Thousands of abandoned children survive in the underground heating tunnels beneath Bucharest and other cities of the collapsed communist economies. Gangs of street children in Brazil maintain themselves by theft and prostitution, and are culled by legally-tolerated death squads (Scanlon *et al.* 1998). In Hong Kong, old people live in 'caged houses', locking themselves in with their remaining possessions. Even in the societies of western Europe and North America, prosperous citizens on their way to work see homeless people sleeping in the doorways of shops, keeping warm around heating ducts, and sheltering under the bridges which carry commuter trains to the cities. Their reaction mixes sympathy and fear, and these same emotions drive public policy. Public funds are allocated to provide temporary accommodation for people sleeping rough, and treatment for those with a mental illness or who misuse substances. But this is often combined with greater police powers to clear the streets and protect the public from the homeless.

Public policy in western Europe and North America has therefore been directed at the 'visible homeless'. Less attention has been paid to the larger number of families and children who become homeless each year, and who are placed in homeless centres or other temporary accommodation provided by local authorities, or who double up with friends and family. This group is diverse, and the reasons that lead to homelessness are complex. Official definitions and policy documents in England usually adopt the statutory definition of 'homelessness', corresponding to the group of individuals or families who are accepted as 'homeless' by local housing authorities. This excludes applicants deemed to have made themselves intentionally homeless, and several groups which are either not identified as priorities for rehousing, or which do not choose to apply to their local housing authority. These groups include single adult rough sleepers and hostel users not referred to local housing authorities; and other groups without stable housing, such as individuals or families doubling up, living in squats, or living as travellers (Williams and Avebury 1995).

Estimates of the number of homeless families and children therefore vary with the definition used. An analysis of official statistics (by Christina Victor, in Chapter 10 of this book) indicates that each year local housing authorities accept about 143,000 families as 'homeless', which include over 170,000 children. To this should be added up to 7000 teenagers living rough or living in hostels. There is a constant turnover in the homeless population, which means that substantially more children experience at least one episode of homelessness before adulthood.

The impact of homelessness on the lives of children and families has received limited attention, although several research studies summarised in this book have found that children in homeless families experience high rates of illness, injury, and distress. The very experience of living in temporary housing can place children at greater risk of accidents and illness, while cramped and transient living circumstances places a strain on family relationships.

The needs of homeless families have received limited attention from policy makers. Homelessness has been seen almost entirely as a housing problem, and there has been limited recognition of the overlaps between the population of homeless families and the populations of children at risk, of children with mental health problems, and of victims of domestic or neighbourhood violence. This book aims to correct this neglect. It brings together researchers in the fields of public health, psychiatry, education, health visiting, social policy, and housing policy, to identify the problems experienced by homeless families and to propose the most effective solutions.

Three initial chapters look at the characteristics of homeless families, focusing particularly on their health needs. Chapter 2, by Stuart Cumella, notes that most of our information about the mental health needs of homeless families derives from a small number of studies, mainly in the USA, of families in homeless centres. He analyses the results from one of the few systematic surveys of families in homeless centres in England (the Birmingham Survey), and confirms the importance of domestic and neighbourhood violence as a key factor leading to homelessness. Chapter 3, by Kath Hutchinson, shows the major risks to the health of children when they are placed by their local authority in bed and breakfast hotels and other poor quality shared accommodation. She reports families living in damp, unventilated rooms, and high rates among children of accidents, infectious diseases, poor nutrition, and developmental delays. Chapter 4, by Panos Vostanis, discusses the impact of homelessness on child mental health, and analyses the underlying mechanisms involved. He reviews the nature of mental health problems among children, and the implications for treatment and services.

The next two chapters consider the association between homelessness and family life. Chapter 5, by Jacqueline Barnes, reviews research on the impact of homelessness on family functioning, and reports results from a qualitative study of bed and breakfast accommodation in London. She found that parents were socially isolated and lacked any source of personal support. They were concerned about the safety of their children, and experienced problems caused by overcrowding and lack of space for the children to play. Nevertheless, many parents showed great resilience and hope for the future. Chapter 6, by Gill Hague and Ellen Malos, looks at the experiences of women who become homeless following domestic violence. They note the lack of protection from the criminal justice system, and consider the possible impact of recent legislative changes in England.

Chapter 7, by Robert Wrate and Caroline Blair, considers the mental health needs of homeless adolescents, and draws upon results from three major studies of this group. They report that about half of homeless adolescents have been in local authority care, and that most have either limited or strained relationships with their family. Rates of mental illness and suicidal thoughts were double those found among the general community.

The next five chapters review access by homeless families to public services. Pat Niner, in Chapter 8, reviews housing policy in England, and shows how the official definition of 'homelessness' has changed since the 1977 Housing (Homeless Persons) Act first placed a duty on local housing authorities to secure accommodation for homeless people who were not intentionally homeless and who had priority need. She notes how definitions of 'priority need' have been implemented, and discusses the 1996 Housing Act which aimed to reduce the priority given to homeless families in allocating social housing. Chapter 9, by Stuart Cumella, returns to the Birmingham Survey, and considers the impact of health, education, and social services on families in homeless centres. He finds that while homeless families were able to access primary health care, few with mental health problems had help from specialist services. Christina R. Victor, in Chapter 10, discusses the problems in estimating the prevalence of homelessness among families. She notes that homeless families are highly mobile, and that this mobility impedes access to effective health care. Chapter 11, by Sally Power, Geoff Whitty, and Deborah Youdell, considers the problems experienced by children in homeless families in maintaining the continuity of their education, and the institutional barriers to developing a more effective service. Chapter 12, by Leila Baker, looks at access to voluntary sector agencies by homeless adolescents, and the problems experienced by non-governmental organisations in providing comprehensive services.

Chapter 13 is by John C. Buckner and Ellen L. Bassuk, who show the confluence of economic and social policy, and demographic factors which have produced a dramatic increase in the number of homeless families in the USA. Their review of recent research confirms the high levels of victimisation and substance misuse among both homeless women and single mothers on welfare benefits, and the high prevalence of mental health problems among both mothers and children in homeless families. They present a picture of a large population of families with single parents, under extreme stress, with little access to stable housing, moving in and out of homeless shelters.

The final chapter draws together the recommendations made by each of the contributing authors, to present a programme of action for professionals and politicians. It is the hope of the editors that this book will stimulate its readers to mobilise the skills and wealth of our society to prevent homelessness wherever possible, to develop effective services and policies for families which do become homeless, and to ensure that homeless families can rapidly return to houses of their own.

CHAPTER 2

Homeless Families

Stuart Cumella

Families in homeless centres

Our knowledge of the mental health of homeless families derives almost entirely from a small number of surveys in homeless centres. Most have been carried out in the USA, where a network of over 2000 centres (termed 'shelters') has developed in the last two decades (Weinreb and Rossi 1995). Despite wide variations in the operation, management, and catchment areas of homeless centres, some consistent results emerge about the characteristics of the families that use them. About three-quarters are headed by an unemployed single mother, and a substantial minority have histories of family breakdown, physical and sexual abuse (both as children and adults), and psychiatric disorders (Bassuk and Browne 1996; Bassuk, Rubin and Lauriat 1986; Cumella, Grattan and Vostanis 1998; Herman *et al.* 1997; North *et al.* 1996; Victor 1992; Vostanis *et al.* 1996; Zima *et al.* 1996).

A few studies have compared families in homeless centres with groups of low income families in settled housing, to identify statistically significant differences which can be interpreted as risk factors for homelessness. Most have found that families in homeless centres have less social support than those in the comparison group. But there is less agreement on the extent to which ethnicity and domestic violence constitute risk factors. Some studies report higher proportions of families from black or minority ethnic groups in homeless centres than among the comparison group of families in settled housing (Bassuk *et al.* 1997), while others have found similar proportions in both groups (Masten *et al.* 1993; Vostanis *et al.* 1997).

As far as domestic violence is concerned, three comparative studies found higher rates among homeless families than among families in settled housing (Bassuk and Rosenberg 1988; Vostanis *et al.* 1997; Wood *et al.* 1990), while two studies found no statistically significant difference (Bassuk *et al.* 1997; Masten *et al.* 1993). The most thorough recent study of risk factors for homelessness among families headed by single mothers found that although the lives of this group had been dominated by violent relationships, the prevalence of lifetime experiences of violence did not differ from that among the comparison group of low income single mothers in settled housing. This led the researchers to conclude that domestic violence did not constitute a risk factor for homelessness among single mothers (Bassuk *et al.* 1997).

Traditional epidemiological models, which essentially involve analysing homelessness as a *quasi*-disease afflicting single mothers, may not be the most appropriate technique for understanding the process which leads from stable

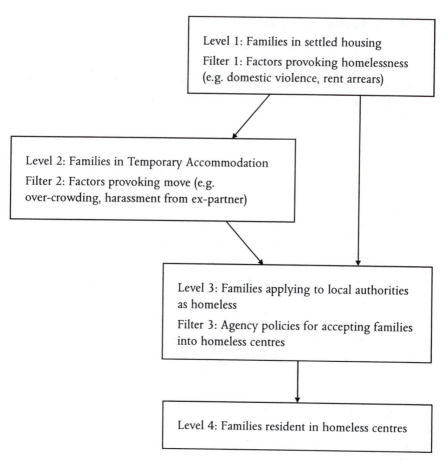

Figure 2.1 Pathways model of admission to homeless centres

housing to homeless centres, and the way this determines the characteristics of families eventually admitted to centres. An alternative is the Pathways Approach, originally developed by Goldberg and Huxley (1980, 1992) to analyse the way in which people are referred to specialist psychiatric services. This distinguishes successive nested 'levels' of population, whose characteristics are determined by the operation of selective 'filters' such as professional and agency policies, the availability and effectiveness of alternative treatment options, and the preferences of people themselves. An application of the pathways approach for families in public homeless facilities is shown in Figure 2.1.

Level 1 in the figure comprises the population in settled housing, from which the homeless population emerges. Filter 1 is the set of circumstances which precipitate homelessness, such as eviction because of rent arrears, or the need to escape domestic violence. Level 2 comprises families in temporary housing, some of whom become a long-term transient population. Filter 2 is the array of circumstances such as overcrowding or harassment from ex-partners which leads families to leave temporary housing and apply to their local authority or non-governmental organisations (NGOs) as homeless. Level 3 is the population which applies to these agencies, while Filter 3 represents agency policies for the acceptance as being an agency responsibility and eligible for admission to a homeless centre. Last, Level 4 comprises the population of families in homeless centres.

The combined operation of each of these filters accounts for the preponderance in homeless centres of families headed by single mothers, particularly those with poor social support. Single-parent families have low median incomes, and are therefore more likely to be at risk of eviction through non-payment of rent or mortgage. In other cases, the loss of stable housing coincides with the creation of a single-parent family, most commonly because the mother and her children flee their home to escape assault from a partner or ex-partner (Filter 1). This group is probably less likely than other homeless families to double up with friends or family (Level 2) because these addresses would be known to their ex-partner. Homeless centres or other refuges are therefore preferred because of their anonymity, and many such families move directly to Level 3. In cases where families do leave stable housing for temporary accommodation, single-parent and other low income families are least likely to have the resources to return to stable housing, and are most likely to be in overcrowded or otherwise unsuitable accommodation. Families with poor social support may even lack any network of family or friends to provide an alternative, however short-term, to admission to a homeless centre.

The operation of Filter 3 may also differentially select homeless families headed by single mothers. Less than a third of homeless applicants to local authorities in England are admitted to any form of temporary accommodation (Charles 1994; O'Callaghan and Dominian 1996), with eligibility determined by statute (reviewed in Chapter 8). Although there have been several statutory and regulatory changes since the original 1977 Housing (Homeless Persons) Act, there has been some consistency in giving priority to people with dependent children who have no accommodation, or where it is unreasonable to remain because of violence or a threat of violence (O'Callaghan and Dominian 1996).

Greater variation in the pathways to homeless centres may occur in countries where there is no consistent statutory entitlement to rehousing for homeless families. A review of homeless centres in the USA found substantial variations in admission criteria, facilities, and the provision of resettlement programmes. The characteristics of families admitted to individual homeless centres were therefore particularly dependent on local selection procedures, and the availability of alternative emergency accommodation in the locality. Many centres in the USA do not provide accommodation for two-parent families, and admission therefore results in parental separation (Weinreb and Rossi 1995).

The Birmingham study

Information about the pathways to homeless centres is available from a longi-tudinal research programme funded by the Nuffield Foundation (described in detail in Cumella et al. 1998; Vostanis et al. 1997; Vostanis, Grattan and Cumella 1998). The main aims of the survey were to identify the extent of mental health problems among homeless families, their ease of access to health, social, and educational services, and the outcome of homelessness in terms of rehousing, and the persistence of mental health problems.

The main sample comprised 168 homeless families with 249 children between the ages of 2 and 16 years who were admitted to homeless centres managed by the City of Birmingham Housing Department over a period of one year. Families with children younger than two years were excluded because there is no reliable way to establish behavioural and emotional problems for this age group. One mother had given birth before admission, and two were expected to give birth shortly, and a further 52 families refused to participate or could not be contacted despite repeated attempts This left 113 families who took part in the research, corresponding to a response rate of 67 per cent. This compares well with other research in homelessness in which the mobility of the survey population prevents high response rates (see, for example, Masten *et al.* 1993). There was no statistically significant difference between respondents and non-respondents in either family structure or homeless centre attended.

The research programme also included interviews with a comparison sample of 29 families with 83 children attending two primary schools in low-income areas of Birmingham. All families in the comparison sample were in settled housing, and had a head of household in the Registrar-General's Social Class V (OPCS 1980). A relatively small comparison sample was selected because of its anticipated social homogeneity and hence low variability, in contrast with the homeless group.

The following research instruments were administered to the mother (or father if sole parent) in both samples:

- *A semi-structured interview* concerning circumstances leading to homelessness (homeless families only), previous family life, peer and family relationships, behavioural problems among the children, and contacts with the health and social services.

- *The Interview Schedule for Social Interaction (ISSI)*. This measured the degree to which homeless families were socially isolated compared with the comparison sample. The ISSI can be used to assess the availability and perceived adequacy of attachment, friendships and acquaintance, the extent of social integration, and satisfaction with social relationships (Henderson *et al.* 1981).

- *The General Health Questionnaire (GHQ)*. This is a standardised screening questionnaire for use in surveys of psychiatric disorders in the general population (Goldberg *et al.* 1976). The 28-item version was used in this study, which generates separate scores for somatic symptoms, anxiety, social dysfunction, and depression. The simple Likert scaling method was used for scoring, for which a total score of 40 or above is used to indicate a mental disorder of clinical significance (Goldberg and Hillier 1979).

The following instruments were completed by the mother (or father if sole parent) for each child in the survey:

- *The Communication Subscale of the Vineland Adaptive Behaviour Scales (VABS)*, which measures the development of communication in children. Scores are adapted according to the norms of the general population, and an age-equivalent score is provided, which indicates the chronological age at which the child is functioning (Sparrow, Bella and Cichetti 1984).

- *The Child Behaviour Checklist (CBCL)*. This has been widely used in research to measure behavioural problems, emotional problems, and social competence (activities, peer-relationships and school performance) in children (Achenbach 1991 and 1992). The CBCL has been standardised in large clinical and non-referred samples. It comprises a rating scale covering symptoms and symptom clusters, and is not a diagnostic measure. However, 'normalised' scores (above 63) have been established to indicate whether the child is within the 'clinical range' (i.e. comparable to children referred for assessment by specialist services). A simpler version of the CBCL was used for children aged between two and three years (Achenbach 1992).

The height and age of each child in the survey was measured by the researcher, and compared with the rest of the general population using the system of age-appropriate centiles (Tanner and Whitehouse 1975) used by children's services at the time of the fieldwork (although these charts have now been superseded). Twenty of the children under the age of 11 years in the sample of homeless families were also interviewed by a child psychiatrist about their experience of family life, school and friends, and living in the hostel.

Follow-up interviews were arranged with both samples approximately one year after first contact, using the same set of research instruments, with modifications to the semi-structured schedule to collect information about duration of residence in the homeless centre and subsequent experiences. Despite the co-operation of the Birmingham Housing and Education Departments, it proved difficult to trace many families. Of the 113 homeless families interviewed in the first stage of the fieldwork, eight had left without any known follow-up address, while a further 28 had moved from a known follow-up address and could not be traced. Twelve had moved away from Birmingham, and seven refused to be re-interviewed. Follow-up interviews were therefore completed with 58 families with 122 children, equivalent to 35 per cent of the original sample and 51 per cent of those interviewed in the

Table 2.1 Characteristics of families in homeless and comparison samples

Characteristic	Homeless Families (%, n = 113)	Comparison Sample (%, n = 29)	Significance levels (note multiple comparisons)
Family composition			
Single mother	85	45	
Single father	4	0	
Both parents	12	55	X^2:p<0.001
Mothers' mean age	30.6 years	32 years	NS
Mother's ethnicity			
White	76	72	
South Asian	13	21	
Afro-Caribbean or African	11	7	NS
Mean age when mother ceased full-time education	15.8 years	16.0 years	NS
Mothers' employment status			
Not employed	93	73	
Part-time work	5	27	
Full-time work	2	0	
Full-time education	1	0	X^2:p<0.001
Median number of children	2	3	NS
ISSI Scores (median and quartiles)			Mann-Whitney U
Availability of attachments	5 (2–7)	7 (6–8)	X^2:p<0.001
Adequacy of attachments	7 (3–10)	10.5 (10–12)	X^2:p<0.001
Availability of social integration	4 (2–7)	9 (8–10.25)	X^2:p<0.001
Adequacy of social integration	12 (8–14)	16 (15–16)	X^2:p<0.001
Rows with attached persons	0 (0–1)	0 (0–0.25)	NS

first phase. The response rate for follow-up interviews with the comparison sample was higher (79%), and included 23 families with 56 children.

Results from the psychiatric measures are described in Chapter 4, while details of contacts with health, social, and educational services are given in Chapter 9. The rest of this chapter will describe the characteristics of the families included in the sample, their path to homeless centres, and the outcome a year later.

Sample characteristics

The characteristics of the families in the homeless and the comparison samples are summarised in Table 2.1. Most (85%) homeless families at the time they were in the homeless centre had a single parent, and the median number of children of all ages was two (range one to six). Three-quarters (76%) of mothers were white, and the majority (89%) of mothers had completed secondary school education, with an average school-leaving age of 15.7 years (range 11 to 19 years). At the time of interview, almost all (93%) mothers of homeless families were not in employment.

There was no statistically significant difference between the homeless and comparison samples with respect to ethnicity, maternal age, number of children, and age at which ceased full-time education. The comparison sample included a higher proportion (55%) of families with both parents, and a higher proportion (27%) of mothers in part-time work. Results from the ISSI indicated that parents in homeless families had lower levels of social integration and fewer attachments than mothers in the comparison sample, and that the perceived quality of their social relationships was poorer.

Pathways to homelessness

Almost all (96%) of the families in the homeless sample had been in stable housing as owners (8%) or tenants (88%) a year before admission to a homeless centre. The remainder were lodging, usually on a long-term basis, with family or friends. The median length of stay in the most recent accommodation before becoming homeless was two years, with a quartile range between eight months and five years.

A small number of families (3%) had been in unstable housing for a prolonged period, involving repeated moves to avoid violent ex-partners or as brief episodic escapes from violent partners. The majority (59%) of families had two parents before they became homeless, while 39 per cent were headed by a single mother and 2 per cent by a single father. There was no statistically significant difference in family status or type of accommodation between the homeless sample in their last stable housing, and the comparison sample.

Almost nine out of ten (89%) families chose to become homeless to escape from violence, either in the form of direct assaults (53%), threats of violence (14%), or from sustained harassment (11%). Smaller numbers left to avoid the sexual or other physical abuse of the children in the family (5%), or following the destruction of household property (5%). Three families became homeless because their house was burnt down by others.

The perpetrators of violence were the current partner (44% of all homeless families), neighbours (27%), ex-partners (25%), and other family members (5%). Direct violence and the abuse of children were most frequently committed by partners, threats of violence by neighbours, and harassment by ex-partners. Causes of homelessness not related to violence included six per cent who were evicted, three per cent who voluntarily left overcrowded accommodation, and two per cent who left because of a (non-violent) relationship problem with members of their household. Some examples of the different causes of homelessness are given in the case vignettes (Boxes 2.1 to 2.6), which have been selected at random from the sample of homeless families.

The majority of families therefore left their last stable housing as a form of escape, which for almost all (90%) two-parent families involved separation of the partners. These circumstances also shaped the choice of alternative accommodation. Many respondents who left home were unwilling to lodge with family of friends because their location would be known to a violent partner or ex-partner. However, a quarter (26%) of families in the homeless sample found their own accommodation after becoming homeless. Two-thirds (67%) of this group lodged with their family or friends, while the remainder found other rented accommodation. Most stayed for only a short period, with a median of six weeks, and an interquartile range between one week and three months. The main reasons for leaving were that the accommodation was overcrowded and occupied on an explicit temporary basis (47%), or because of continued assault from ex-partners (37%).

Families in homeless centres

When interviewed, most parents and children were appreciative of the homeless centre and its staff. Those who had become homeless following domestic or neighbourhood violence welcomed the security it provided. The reports

---

Box 2.1 Case Study A

At the time of the initial interviews, Alison was a single mother in her early thirties with two sons aged seven and three. The younger has a speech problem, and was described by Alison as 'hyperactive'. Alison had lived for seven years in a council flat before becoming homeless. This followed fighting between her children and those of her upstairs neighbour, who eventually physically attacked her and hit her son on the head with a brick.

After moving to the homeless centre, her elder son moved to a new school near the homeless centre. No place was available in a nursery school for the younger son, who attended a playgroup next door to the homeless centre. Alison arranged for them to visit their friends at weekends. The experience of homelessness affected her two sons differently. The older one had become much quieter, but was happy to be away from the fighting, while his younger brother became more hyperactive. Both had CBCL scores in the clinical range. None of the family had been in contact with social services, educational psychologists, or any mental health services.

When interviewed in the homeless centre, Alison said she hoped to find a settled home, and improve her employment prospects by doing a course at a college.

Alison spent three months in the homeless centre, and accepted the second house offered. At follow-up, Alison was living in a rented house in a different part of the City, and said she was very happy with her new house. She reported that both sons had settled since rehousing, and both were below the clinical threshold on the CBCL. Neither had missed any schooling, and both had succeeded in making new friends.

---

in Box 2.7 are representative. Parents were concerned with the lack of space and the need for the entire family to share a single room. This could make it difficult to maintain bed-time routines, and several parents reported problems in getting their children to sleep at night. The lack of play space in any of the centres became a particular problem in winter (when outdoor play is less possible), resulting in the need for parents to spend 24 hours a day in the company of their children. Although the Housing Department policy is to rehouse families within 28 days, some stays in homeless centres became much longer. This sometimes resulted in extremely strained family relationships.

Box 2.2 Case Study B

At the time of the initial interview, Becky was an Afro-Caribbean woman in her mid-twenties who worked as a part-time administrator. She had a medical history of hypertension, which had led to a premature Caesarian delivery of her daughter, now nine years. The daughter herself had frequent chest infections and delayed speech development.

Before becoming homeless, she had lived in a house owned by a Housing Association for six years. This was rat-infested, and had rotting floorboards, faulty electrics, and mould growing on the walls. She withheld her rent until the Housing Association agreed to repairs, but was evicted for non-payment. She moved in with her mother, initially on an emergency basis. Becky had always had a strained relationship with her mother, but this deteriorated further when they were in the same house, leading to arguments and imposed curfews. After four months, Becky was eventually evicted by her mother, and moved to live with her brother and his family. But space was limited, and she left after two weeks.

After becoming homeless, her daughter continued to attend the same school and go to the same Brownie pack. Nevertheless, she had become moody and aggressive, refused food, had wet the bed, and cried a lot. She now became distressed when her mother was out of view, and refused to go to the toilet unless the door was left open and she could see her mother. Her CBCL score was in the clinical range. She had been in contact with an educational psychologist before becoming homeless, and a social worker when in the homeless centre.

At the time of the initial interview, Becky had a General Health Questionnaire score in the clinical range. She hoped to be settled once again in a new house in the City, continuing in the same employment, and with her daughter attending the same school.

Becky spent six months in a homeless centre, and refused several offers of rehousing. She eventually moved to a council flat, which she had exchanged with a council house by the time of the follow-up interviews. She was 'quite satisfied' with her new house.

The daughter had not missed any schooling despite being homeless, and had remained in the same school. Becky reported that her daughter had settled down, and her CBCL score at follow-up had fallen and was now below the clinical threshold. Becky herself was now below the clinical threshold on the GHQ.

Box 2.3 Case Study C

At the time of the initial interview, Corinne was a single mother in her thirties, with a ten-year-old daughter, and an eight-year-old son who had a history of asthma.

Corinne had lived in a violent relationship with her partner for nine years, until she left to escape assault and became homeless. She was re-housed in a council house in another part of the City, and began a new relationship. Her new partner became increasingly aggressive, and one day struck her and broke her jaw. Having previous experience of long-term violent relationships, Corinne decided to leave immediately, but was unable to move in with her parents because of lack of space.

While in the homeless centre, Corinne made no arrangements for her children to attend school or to see their friends. She described their behaviour as normal but bored. However, her son was above the clinical range on the CBCL. Corinne herself hoped to become settled in a new house, and return to her studies at a local college.

Corinne was in the homeless centre for five months and accepted the first property offered. This was owned by a housing association and she was dissatisfied with her house because it was scheduled for demo-lition. Nevertheless, she felt that things had improved for the children who were now both at school (although they had missed five months' education). Both were now below the clinical threshold for the CBCL.

After homelessness

Results from the follow-up stage showed that the median length of stay in a homeless centre before being offered a permanent residence was eight weeks (range 3 to 10). Three-quarters (74%) accepted the first property offered by the Housing Department. A significant minority (23%) of those interviewed had moved house again, including 10 per cent who became homeless once more. At the time of the follow-up interviews, 90 per cent were living in rented property, 5 per cent were owner-occupiers, and 5 per cent were home-less. Most (68%) parents were 'very' or 'quite satisfied' with their current house, and almost three-quarters (73%) were 'very' or 'quite satisfied' with the area in which they lived.

These levels of satisfaction were not significantly different from those found among the comparison group of families. The survey did not collect

---

Box 2.4 Case Study D

At the time of the initial interviews, Denise was a woman in her late twenties with a seven-year-old son and a four-year-old daughter.

Denise had lived with her fiancé in an owner-occupied house for five years before becoming homeless. During this time, she had been increasingly harassed by her prospective father-in-law, who lived nearby. When he had eventually threatened to beat her up, she found that her fiancé refused to defend her or confront his parents. She decided to leave until her fiancé agreed to her demand that they break off contact with his father. Denise was unable to move in with her sister, who had seven children, and therefore chose to become homeless.

When interviewed, she said both children had become very 'clingy', and followed her constantly. Her son moved to a new school near the homeless centre, while her daughter ceased attending nursery school. The daughter was above the clinical threshold on the CBCL.

When in the homeless centre, Denise said she hoped to be settled in her own home, and find a part-time job. She remained in the centre for 12 weeks, and accepted the first property offered. When interviewed a year later, she said she was very satisfied with her new home. Neither child had missed any schooling, and, according to their mother, had 'no problems'. Nevertheless, the son was just above the CBCL clinical threshold, although the daughter was no longer in the clinical range.

---

information about family income, but 14 per cent of mothers in the homeless sample were working (almost all part-time), compared with 35 per cent of mothers in the comparison sample. Many single mothers planned to improve their employment prospects through vocational training, as can be seen in some of the case vignettes.

For many families contacted, homelessness involved a transition from living in a violent relationship with a partner, to living in their own home as a single parent. But by the follow-up interviews, 33 per cent of families had two parents, including 12 per cent who had remained as a couple throughout the experience of homelessness, 12 per cent who had returned to their former partner, and 9 per cent who had found a new partner since leaving the homeless centre. More than four in five homeless parents interviewed at the

---

Box 2.5 Case Study E

When first interviewed, Eleanor was a woman in her forties, who had lived with her husband, three sons (aged 17, 13 and 9), and a daughter (aged 16) in the same council house for the last four years. There had been a history of regular arguments and violence from her husband for many years, and she eventually decided to leave after a fight broke out between her husband and her eldest son.

This occurred during the school holidays, and when interviewed, Eleanor had yet to make any arrangements for the children to continue to attend school. She believed that the experience of homelessness had not been too bad for the children. However, the 13-year-old son (who she said had a history of asthma and temper tantrums) was above the clinical threshold on the CBCL. Eleanor hoped to return to her own home after the council had evicted her husband.

Eleanor remained in the homeless centre for nine months before her husband had been evicted and she could return to her old home. By then, her daughter had missed seven months schooling, while the two sons still of school age had missed three months each. Although Eleanor continued to state that homelessness had not affected her children, she said the oldest son was now quiet and withdrawn, while her second oldest son had behaviour problems and continued to be above the clinical threshold on the CBCL.

---

follow-up believed their life had improved in the last year (84%), and that the lives of their children had improved (83%).

Conclusion

The results reported in this chapter suggest that the characteristics of families in homeless centres are determined by a complex process of selection, involving the policies of national government and individual housing agencies, the availability of alternative emergency accommodation, and the decision made by homeless families themselves. For most families, becoming homeless was a successful form of problem solving, albeit in extreme circumstances including threatened loss of life. Becoming homeless and being rehoused eventually improved the lives of most of the parents interviewed in the follow-up survey, but at the cost of losing their household property, living in cramped accommodation in a homeless centre, and disrupting the

Box 2.6 Case study F

At the time of the initial interview, Fiona was a woman in her late twenties with a seven-year-old daughter and a two-year-old son. Both children had had difficult births. Her daughter had hearing problems and was described as 'hyperactive'. The son had had previous hospital admissions for various disorders.

Before becoming homeless, she had been married for five years, and had lived with her husband in a council house. The relationship between them had been deteriorating for the previous two years because of her husband's drinking sessions, which often involved threats of violence. Her response in the past had been to leave home and stay with her mother, but she had always gone back. She had become more depressed, and decided to leave for good after her husband became very drunk one day, and threatened to kill her.

When interviewed, Eleanor said she felt guilty about the situation the children were now in. She was unable to sleep at night and had a score on the GHQ above the clinical threshold. She had visited a GP near the homeless centre, who had diagnosed postnatal depression, and arranged for a CPN (community psychiatric nurse) to visit. Her daughter continued to attend the same school, even though this involved an hour's travel each way. Eleanor had not told the school about the change in circumstances, because she felt 'it was none of their business'. Eleanor had told her daughter that the homeless centre was a hotel, and had asked her if they should return to their home. The daughter had replied 'No. You just fight'.

When asked about her hopes for the future, Eleanor said she wanted to enrol in college and train for a job which involves working with children, and settle in a new home of her own with new friends. She went to a women returners' course when at the homeless centre, during which time her son attended a creche next door.

Eleanor was in the homeless centre for six weeks, before accepting the first house offered. She said she was quite satisfied with her new home, and that her daughter had settled at her new school. She believed that being homeless had not affected them very much. She was no longer above the clinical threshold for the GHQ.

Box 2.7 Children's views of the homeless centre

I like the hostel because there are locks on all the doors, so nobody can get us. I don't like it because you're not allowed to be naughty. There's nowhere to play, except in here or outside (five-year-old boy).

The best thing about the hostel is that I can stay in bed. It's better here because those people won't find us and beat us up. I've made friends here with the girl downstairs. We like to play hide and seek or football (seven-year-old girl).

I like the hostel. We watch telly or play pogs, or go out in the back garden to play football. The people are nice – they treat you well. It's a better place than home. Mom doesn't cry any more (seven-year-old boy).

I was mad about coming to the hostel. We shouldn't have been the ones that had to move. (seven-year-old girl).

I miss the garden at home. I had loads of friends at home. I miss them too (five-year-old boy).

friendships and schooling of their children. However, there was a small group at the follow-up stage who had repeat experiences of homelessness and had not found settled housing. The size of this group may be under-estimated in the research because the high number of non-respondents for the follow-up interviews may include many who could not be contacted because they had no settled home.

These results re-affirm the importance of violence (from partners, ex-partners, and neighbours) as a key determinant of homelessness among families passing through homeless centres. This may be masked in official housing statistics because some families who enter homeless accommodation after a short period lodging with family or friends have factors such as overcrowding recorded as the immediate cause of homelessness (O'Callaghan and Dominian 1996). A similar process may account for variations between different research studies in the extent to which they identify domestic violence as a risk factor for homelessness. Those which found equivalent levels of domestic violence between homeless and comparison samples (Bassuk *et al.* 1997; Masten *et al.* 1993) have included a substantial proportion of homeless families who had been in Level 2 housing before admission to homeless centres, for whom domestic violence may have played an important part in the initial loss of stable Level 1 housing. However, further analysis is needed to clarify this issue.

The results from the Birmingham Study emphasise the importance of the continued provision of homeless centres as clean and safe emergency accommodation for families. Homeless centres, and the network of other refuges for victims of domestic violence provide a sanctuary and may have saved the lives of many women and children at risk from violent partners, ex-partners, or neighbours. The problems reported by homeless families indicate a need for trained and skilled support staff in homeless centres, and for indoor and outdoor play facilities for children.

Nevertheless, homeless centres are only suitable for short-term accommodation, and both central government and local housing authorities need a clear policy commitment to provide rapid and permanent rehousing for homeless families, to minimise the risk of personal and family breakdown. This requires a change in UK government policy, which since the early 1980s has opposed the provision of public rented housing, culminating in the 1996 Housing Act which deprived homeless families of an entitlement to rehousing in permanent accommodation.

Providing alternative emergency accommodation and subsequent rehousing, although essential, is a second best option for families which have become homeless as a result of domestic or neighbourhood violence. A key objective of public policy should be the prevention of homelessness from these causes. The results reported in this paper confirm that most families entered homeless centres following an apparent failure of the criminal justice system to protect them from systematic and repeated violence from known perpetrators. Since the research reviewed in this chapter, there have been a number of changes in English law, designed to give greater protection to victims of abuse or harassment, and these are reviewed in Chapter 6.

CHAPTER 3

Health Problems
of Homeless Children

Kath Hutchinson

Health and homeless families

'Health' was described by the World Health Organization in 1946, as a state of complete physical, mental and social well-being (WHO 1946). This indicates that health is more than freedom from disease (Calnan 1987). Seedhouse (1986) added dimension to the meaning of health suggesting that it refers to the availability of the means to achieve one's full potential and is related to quality of life. Blaxter (1990) suggests that socio-economic factors, external circumstances and the psychosocial environment are more accurate determinants of health than the practice of healthy or unhealthy behaviour. Daly (1989) recognises that homelessness is associated with a variety of problems which have direct bearing on health. The range of social, environmental, psychological, and financial disadvantage is such that all Blaxter's (1990) determinants of health are compromised and the opportunities to aspire to Seedhouse's definition of health are removed.

The West Berkshire study

In 1992, the West Berkshire Priority Care Service (a National Health Service community trust) seconded a specialist health visitor to identify the specific health needs of homeless families and to facilitate access to health and welfare services (Hutchinson and Gutteridge 1995). Of the 148 families encountered that year, 61 per cent had a lone mother as head of the household. Most of the parents were young, almost half (49%) being aged less than 22 years and a third (33%) aged between 23 to 28 years.

The proportion of families of ethnic minority origin was 20 per cent, double that of the general population of the town. The rate of unemployment and dependency on state benefit, among parents, was 89 per cent. Of the employed all but two people (9%) had jobs that placed them in the Registrar General's lower socio-economic groups. People from cultural minorities may have limited access to health care (Karmi 1993).Those in low socio-economic groups, as shown by the Black report, have poorer health than those in higher groups (Townsend and Davidson 1982), factors which are further compromised by homelessness. This chapter draws on the results from the West Berkshire, and from case studies reported in Hutchinson (1997).

Temporary accommodation

Children and families may be placed in temporary accommodation by local authorities, who have a duty to house them but do not have permanent accommodation available. Families which do not meet the statutory require-ments for priority housing may themselves move to hostels, mobile homes, refuges, temporary bungalows, private sector short-term leased property or bed and breakfast hotels. Other types of temporary accommodation include probation or bail hostels.

The poverty of environment was highlighted by the Child Accident Prevention Trust (1991), which found that most temporary accommodation used by local authorities in the United Kingdom was 'ill designed, ill equipped and ill maintained' (p.5). One type of temporary accommodation used by some housing authorities, also leased by some hidden homeless families, is a private sector house of multiple occupation. This is a house occupied by persons who do not form a single household, and includes a variety of arrangements from bed-sits with cooking facilities in rooms (where tenants share bathrooms), to individually let rooms (where kitchens, bathrooms and living rooms are shared). Many such houses of multiple occupation are still in use in parts of the UK, despite, in 1986, being found to be the worst type of housing (Thomas and Hedges 1986).

Accidents

The poor design of much shared and temporary accommodation can put child safety at risk. Features which increase the likelihood of accidents to children include unsafe windows, inappropriate cooking and heating arrangements, overcrowding, shortage of space, lack of safe outdoor play areas, living on upper floors which necessitates much use of stairs, and a general state of disrepair (Child Accident Prevention Trust 1991). Where families have to carry hot food from a communal kitchen – or, in order to avoid this, improvise a means of cooking in their own rooms – scalds and burns are frequent (Families in Bayswater Bed and Breakfast 1987).

Box 3.1 Accident risk

Mr and Mrs Jones were not able to use the cooker in the communal kitchen, because there had been a gas leak and the supply had been disconnected. They were lent a portable cooker, which they placed on a work surface in their room. The surface was not strong enough to support the unit and became loose whilst a pan of hot fat was on the stove. The pan slipped off and their small daughter was burnt with the hot fat.

Linda would not take Harry, her ten-month-old son, to the communal kitchen because of the dirty state left by others. To protect him from the dangers of falling on the stairs and from spilling of hot food, she nailed an improvised gate across the doorway to keep him in the room. At meal times she collected utensils and food, climbed over the gate, descended two flights of stairs and hastily heated the food before making the reverse journey. Although he was protected from falls and scalds on the stairs he was often distressed at being left and exposed to dangers by being alone in the room.

Accidents to children remain a serious concern. In 1991, 543 children under the age of five years died in England as a result of accidents (Department of Health 1992). More than 6000 children die each year in the European Union, with falls and burns being a common causes of fatalities at home (National Children's Home Action for Children 1996). Although it may be perceived that parents are not aware of child safety, the reverse was found by Davies (1992), who discovered that parents were aware of dangers but did not have control in the shared environment. Other tenants might fail to close outside doors or cause other hazards. The risks are greater where children and families are placed with vulnerable people who may not be familiar with the safety needs of children.

Box 3.2 Risks from other residents

Tom, Jane and their four children, two of whom were below school age, were placed in a bed and breakfast hotel. Miriam, a middle-aged woman, recovering from manic-depressive illness, was in the same hotel. Miriam had a habit of cleaning and frequently left buckets of bleach and other strong cleaning substances within the children's reach. She also caused distress by repeatedly opening the door of the room occupied by the two school-age children, at night (Hutchinson 1992).

The Child Accident Prevention Trust (1991) also found that parents were aware of the dangers but were prevented from taking steps to address the risks, due to poverty and the temporary nature of the accommodation.

The cost of safety equipment may be too high for those on state benefit, who might also reason that it would be unwise to purchase equipment which may not fit their next home. Thus the traditional advice and information giving health promotion activity (Robertson 1991) would be unlikely to increase the use of such equipment and might even compound parents feelings of inadequacy. A self-empowering strategy (Billingham 1991) may be more effective in changing behaviour. Such a strategy is employed in schemes where practitioners acquire funding to purchase safety equipment such as stair gates and window locks at low cost, the savings being passed on to families who can buy equipment at a substantial saving on retail price (Hutchinson 1996).

In addition to the increased risk of accident to children in temporary accommodation, there is also greater risk of fire. A survey of houses in multiple occupation (HMSO 1985) revealed that 80 per cent had inadequate means of fire escape. The overcrowding, inadequate electric wiring, inappropriate cooking facilities and poor maintenance of houses of multiple occupation and other shared accommodation increases the risk of fire to ten times that of a family in ordinary housing (National Consumer Council 1992). Even where fire regulations have been observed, the author knows hostels that do not have secure outer doors and are subject to vandalism, exposing tenants to risks associated with damaged electrical fittings, empty fire extinguishers and broken smoke alarms.

To address the disrepair that is potentially dangerous for children in houses of multiple occupation, it is necessary for practitioners to liaise closely with environmental health officers who have a duty to inspect and enforce standards. Without sufficient knowledge of their role and without close liaison, health visitors or other community nurses may fail to make appropriate referrals or may fail to reach the appropriate environmental health officer. A system to remedy these problems, initially devised by health visitors and environmental health officers in Oxford, has been adapted for use in a number of towns (Child Accident Prevention Trust 1992). Practitioners are provided with a checklist of property defects, for which the environmental officer can take legal action. On finding such defects, the nurse can consult the list, advise if action can be taken, mark the relevant section of the checklist, which is then sent to the environmental officer, who will arrange to make a full inspection of the property.

Where a health authority employs a specialist health visitor or other practitioner to address the needs of homeless families, liaison with other agencies, including the environmental health department, should be included in the role. Supporting the work of other practitioners by the distribution of information or facilities that improve access to services for the client group, such as this checklist, should also be undertaken by the specialist health worker.

Cold, damp and mould growth

In hotels and other houses in multiple occupation, ventilation is likely to be poor. A window is usually the only means of ventilation, yet many windows open at a low level or on to unsafe balconies. Thomas and Niner (1989) found that one third of windows in accommodation used for children could not be opened safely. Central heating may be controlled by a property manager and may be set at a low level or turned off at certain times.

Poor ventilation, poor heating and crowding of temporary environments may lead to condensation on cold walls, which can cause them to become damp and support mould growth (Drennan and Stearn 1986). The presence of damp increases the prevalence of viral and bacterial organisms that cause infections (Kingdom 1960). Mould growth has been shown to be associated with allergy and respiratory infections (Platt, Martin and Hunt 1989), which homeless children often suffer from (Drennan and Strearn 1986). The findings of Platt, Martin and Hunt (1989) were shown to be relevant irrespective of income, cooking and washing facilities or smoking in the household. However, logic dictates that damp and mould growth might be exacerbated by excess condensation where families in temporary accommodation cook and dry laundry in a crowded living area.

In addition, children in homeless families might be more exposed to the dangers of passive smoking. The association between caring and smoking was shown in the General Household Survey of 1992 (OPCS), which revealed that over a third (37%) of young, married women aged 16 to 24 are cigarette smokers, compared to a rate of one quarter (26%) among those without children. Graham (1993) reveals that smoking is more prevalent amongst lone, rather than cohabiting or married mothers, and suggests that women's smoking is linked to their coping with heavy caring loads in materially deprived circumstances.

The task of caring is particularly arduous for mothers of homeless families and to due to the high prevalence of young, lone mothers (Hutchinson 1992), overcrowding and cramped living conditions, homeless children are more likely to be exposed to the effects of passive smoking than the general population.

Infections

Stearn (1986) found diarrhoea and vomiting to be common in houses in multiple occupation due to inadequate water supply and shared sanitation. For reasons stated earlier, communal kitchens in bed and breakfast hotels and other houses in multiple occupation may be avoided by tenants. Where families do not have use of a refrigerator, food may be eaten after it has started to deteriorate. If there is no cupboard space in rooms, cooking utensils and packaged food may be stored on open surfaces or on floors, where there could be infestation by mice (Davies 1992). Poor cleaning of crockery and cooking utensils in wash hand basins, which are inadequate for that purpose, may also increase the risk of gastro-intestinal infections, and water drawn from such sources may not be suitable for drinking.

Because of the crowding in shared households, viral illness spreads quickly (Victor 1992), causing homeless children to be more susceptible to viral infections. Air-borne infections are passed from one individual to another by coughing, shouting, laughing or sneezing (Gibson 1959). Infection spreads more quickly where there is crowding, poor ventilation, poor natural lighting and damp (Gibson 1959), conditions which often exist in temporary accommodation (Child Accident Prevention Trust 1991).

The rate of infectious illness in homeless children in shelters in New York was found to be much higher than that of the general population (Rafferty and Shinn 1991). In Reading, Davies (1992) found that 66 per cent of children, in shared temporary accommodation, had experienced acute upper respiratory infection in a four week period. Whereas in the general population 11 per cent of 2 to 4 year olds and 12 per cent of 5 to 15 years olds had experienced acute illness, which restricted their usual activity, in a two-week period (OPCS 1992).

Droplets of moisture containing the infective organism may be inhaled or may fall on to clothing, furnishings, bedding or crockery, where they dry leaving an infectious dust. Chicken pox, scarletina, influenza and the common cold can be contracted this way. Protection from some air-borne infections can be afforded by the children's immunisation programme, including diphtheria, whooping cough, poliomyelitis, a common form of meningitis, measles, mumps, rubella and tuberculosis. The incidence of tuberculosis has risen among street homeless in the UK and in the USA (Griffiths-Jones 1997). Where street homeless adults are accepted for housing because they are found to be vulnerable, the practice of placing such applicants with families might lead to children being exposed to the disease.

In order to protect the population from these diseases, immunisation rates need to be high, yet homelessness may lead to difficulty in compliance with the immunisation programme. Families in shared accommodation may have a communal letter box where mail, including appointments for immunisation or routine assessments, could be defaced, lost or stolen. The frequent and quick change of accommodation may result in appointments arriving after a family has moved.

During an initial secondment, the specialist health visitor found that almost 25 per cent of families had children whose immunisation programme was behind schedule (Hutchinson 1992). The appropriate primary health care teams were informed of the change in circumstances and new immunisation appointments were issued. An inspection of the central child health records eight weeks later revealed that all those remaining in the area had resumed the programme. This activity served as a pilot for a local notification system, one of many that are now in place in different areas (Firth 1995). Such schemes involve local homeless agencies, with tenants' permission, notifying health authorities of the change of address of families who move or are placed in temporary accommodation. The new address is notified to the named health visitor for pre-school-age children, school nurse for school-age children and midwife for expectant mothers.

The notification allows the named nurse to amend databases ensuring that routine appointments for immunisation and health assessments reach the correct destination. Arrangements can be made to transfer the family to local primary health care staff if they move to a new area. Specialist agencies can be notified so that they too can ensure that both correspondence and practitioners arrive at the correct address. When information is incomplete or when they are not registered appropriately, the specialist health care worker can visit and be the named nurse until the family register locally. In this way, gaps in care can be avoided, continuity and consistency of care protected and the family given any necessary information about services in their new area. This practice is described by Jezewski (1995), who used the phrase 'staying connected' (p.205) to illustrate the practice of nurses establishing links with homeless clients, maintaining networks with other providers and arranging access to health care services.

Child development

Some effects of homelessness on child development are discussed in the next chapter. However, the mobility of the population and the traditional role of institutions to support static populations may disguise problems. Drennan and Stearn (1986) found that gross motor and language development of pre-school-age children were delayed, due emotionally to the low self-esteem of parents, and physically to there being limited indoor play space and absence of safe outdoor space. Psychological stress in this age group was shown by the high incidence of behaviour problems (Drennan and Stearn 1986). High mobility prevents continuing care. A new practitioner may accurately assess a child's current state but, not having met the family before, may not identify regression of development or extent of behaviour change, which might indicate the level of psychological distress. School-age children are disadvantaged educationally by mobility and frequent change of school, and the stigma of homelessness (Her Majesty's Inspectorate of Schools 1990), which again may not be easily identified by practitioners newly meeting a child (see Chapter 10). Reimer, Van Cleve and Gilbraith (1995) also found that changing to new practitioners was a factor contributing to poor access to preventive health services for children under 13 years from homeless families in southern California.

Box 3.3 Disruption to schooling

A mother of a five-year-old boy in the UK said:

> Since he started school last September, this is his third school. He's got a lack of self-confidence, and he's easily distracted. Because he's never actually settled in to a school routine, and because he entered when all the other children had already formed their peer groups, it's made him not so confident. He's on the outside and not able to push himself forward. There's things like his bed wetting and his anxiety and him not knowing the future. Its very hard for him to feel secure knowing that we've got to move again soon.

Access to services

Although the incidence of illness in homeless people has been shown to be higher than that of the general population, access to health care is likely to be poorer. Because homelessness usually occurs with little warning, families need accommodation urgently. They therefore have to accept whatever is offered, which may be some distance from their former home and from their familiar general practitioner, and they may not know where to find local services or information.

Box 3.4 Isolation from familiar services

Ms S and her three-month-old baby became homeless when their tenancy agreement expired. Their local council had no vacant property, so they were offered temporary accommodation in another town. Not knowing the town, Ms S took a taxi from the bus station. It was becoming dark when they arrived, so Ms S saw little on the journey and was left at the accommodation not knowing where to go to find a shop, a clinic or any medical services.

Having just experienced the trauma of becoming homeless, immediate attention might be focused on securing a means of providing nourishment, warmth and basic essentials, rather than registering for medical care (Health Visitors' Association and General Medical Services Council 1989). The specialist health visitor found that almost 40 per cent of families that had moved house remained registered with a general practitioner near their former home, and 30 per cent had a general practitioner who was based in another town (Hutchinson 1992).

Although parents in the UK are given a parent-held child health record by their health visitor, 20 per cent of homeless families had lost the record when changing temporary accommodation address (Hutchinson 1992). Such records, if available, are very useful for families who change address, because it can take a number of months for medical records to be forwarded or, if families only register as temporary patients in the new area, records are not sent on.

Box 3.5 Problems with maintaining child health records

The mother of a traveller family, who had been unable to keep her child records up to date said: 'Moving around the whole time, we didn't have a proper health visitor, proper doctor and that. We were going from doctor to doctor, half of them don't know what you're doing. An' if they get sick when we're out travelling, we have to go to the hospital (Accident and Emergency Department) to get medicine'.

This problem with health records might not be resolved until electronic record keeping becomes universal. However, access to health care can be improved by primary health care services being sufficiently flexible to meet the requirements of temporary residents, without their being made to feel inferior, and by being tolerant enough to understand the difficulties of the client group, so that they might be sympathetically accommodated.

The high rate of anxiety and depression in homeless parents (Drennan and Stern 1986) may contribute to the inability to be proactive in seeking health care, when being asked to move to temporary accommodation in another area. The high dependence of mothers in lower socio-economic groups on their own mothers and extended families was shown by Young and Willmot (1957), and later confirmed by Willmott (1986), who found that family and close friends gave help, advice and support. When families make the effort to secure health care, access to services can still be difficult.

Where not precluded for safety reasons, placing families in accommodation close to their former home might allow them to remain with familiar

---

Box 3.6 Problems accessing services

A mother of four children, who had been placed in temporary accommodation within the same town said: 'I went to my old doctor's and they wouldn't see us because we'd moved out of the area. When I went up to a new doctor's, they wouldn't see us straight away because we hadn't registered with them, so it's taken a good month for us to get health care'.

---

practitioners and support networks. However, placements are usually made urgently and this may not be possible. Notification systems, described earlier, will ensure that families are contacted in their new areas but information is not transferred immediately and practitioners may not be able to respond on the day of notification. It would be of value, therefore, if housing authorities could liaise with health and welfare agencies and produce information sheets, including how to access health services, for those being moved to a new area. In areas where there are specialist practitioners for homeless people, this might be part of their role.

Accessing infant immunisation and general health care can be particularly difficult for travellers, who have among the highest levels of morbidity and mortality in the UK (Anderson 1997). Because of the Criminal Justice and Public Order Act in the UK (HMSO 1994), they may be required to move on when asked to within a number of hours or risk prosecution. In some rural areas, where there are recognised sites, there are specialist multi-skilled health workers that work with the client group and bring services such as immunisation to the travellers' homes (Gammon 1996).

In city areas where there are no designated sites, travellers may arrive and be moved on without health workers being aware of this. Perhaps specialist homeless workers could build links with the relevant environmental and law enforcement agencies so that health workers would know when travellers arrived. A multi-skilled health worker or nurse practitioner could be deployed to respond quickly and use knowledge of local agencies in order to secure fast delivery of necessary services. It is also likely that this practitioner would find it necessary to represent to authorities the health and environmental needs of families. Bunce (1996) suggests that health care workers need to be involved in influencing authorities to provide sites that have basic amenities such as drinking water and rubbish disposal. These practices are consistent with the radico-political model of health promotion described by Billingham (1991).

Nutrition

Lack of cooking facilities or theft of food from communal fridges (Davies 1992), may lead families to depend on take-away foods.

Box 3.7 Problems with communal kitchens

One mother, prior to becoming accepted as homeless by the local authority, had lived in a house in multiple occupation. The other tenants were all men who left the kitchen in a dirty state. The woman who was pregnant soon realised that she was the only one cleaning the kitchen and taking the rubbish out. She said: 'One time I decided I wasn't going to do it an' see if someone else was going to do it, and nobody did it. In the end, there were maggots coming out of the bin. I didn't want my child brought up there. I went to the council'.

Good quality take-away foods may be expensive and beyond the means of low income families. Cheaper filling foods, such as fried potato chips or pre-cooked pies and sausage rolls, tend to be high in fat content and low in protein and fibre. Drennan and Stearn (1986) found that children and adults in bed and breakfast accommodation were malnourished. The effects of such poor nutrition on pregnant women was shown by Conway (1988), who found a high incidence of anaemia amongst pregnant women staying in hotels. The effects on children were demonstrated by examination of health records, which showed that 25 per cent of babies born to mothers staying in bed and breakfast accommodation had a birth weight less than 2500 grammes, which was double the incidence of birth weights below 2500 grammes in control groups (Parsons 1991).

Such low birth weight, in relation to gestational age, increases the risk of congenital handicaps and reduces the likelihood of experiencing a healthy young life (Conway 1988). The effects of poor nutrition in mothers may render them unable to breast feed their infants, increasing the risk of infection due to reduced maternal antibody acquisition and to inadequate facilities for preparation of infant formula feeds. Traditional publications on dietary requirements of the expectant mother or well balanced diet for children and adults may have little relevance for families who are on low incomes and have poor cooking and food storage facilities. Recent research has revealed that parents are aware of what foods their children need and will provide them to the best of their ability, often to the detriment of their own needs.

Box 3.8 The cost of good food

One mother of two small children said:

> Everything's very expensive, you wanna try and give them good healthy food. Sometimes you can do that cheaply, but things do cost a lot of money, and it's hard, but I mean you know how expensive fruit is. You know, I can only afford to buy either apples or bananas or oranges. I can never buy it all in one week, and fruit is something I like to have a lot of, because I would eat a lot, but I can never seem to afford to do so. I try to make sure I've got a dinner meal for every day. Sometimes I don't eat enough, then come lunch time or early evening I feel a bit dizzy an' I realise I've got to eat something.

Poverty

The disadvantage of this client group is further compromised by poverty. Ninety-five per cent of the families visited by the specialist health visitor (Hutchinson 1994) were dependent on state benefit. Further to this, 66 per cent of the homeless families (Hutchinson 1994) were headed by a lone parent and therefore, likely to remain in poverty for a number of years (Oppenheim and Harker 1996). Because of the high cost of child care, lone parents are unlikely to earn sufficient money to meet all their financial needs and are therefore likely to remain dependent on state benefit for long periods. State benefit is claimed to be set too low to maintain family health and restricts the ability to make healthy choices in relation to environment, diet, housing, clothing, leisure or any aspect of life (Blackburn 1991).

Poverty is extremely acute in children of asylum seekers who fail to declare their intention on arrival in the UK. This group are not entitled to housing or state benefits (HMSO 1996) and can be supported at subsistence level by social service departments, under the terms of the Children's Act (HMSO 1989). Although adequate affordable housing of a decent standard is needed to remove child homelessness and the associated health risks, permanent housing alone may not remove the trauma of homelessness and the associated social exclusion and disempowerment.

Families may need help to find low cost furniture, claim social security grants or loans or to make charity requests. They will also need information and introduction to local services and agencies such as local health services, social services, education and voluntary support agencies in order to be integrated back into community life. This process of resettlement might be more effective if the family's housing needs are linked to a health needs assessment before rehousing, and if statutory and voluntary agencies work collectively to achieve this aim (Collard 1997).

Recommendations

- Government housing, economic, and social policies should ensure that all families have access to decent, affordable accommodation.
- Multi-agency forums are needed to inform agencies of each others' role.
- Key personnel from each agency should inform and support the work of their own discipline and work jointly on projects to:
  - adapt or develop systems to access services (such as the environmental health officer checklist or notifications of change of address)
  - compile and distribute information on local statutory and voluntary agencies, special support services, and low cost purchase schemes; monitor need
  - address unmet need.
- Health care systems and personnel should take account of the practical difficulties associated with homelessness and be more flexible and tolerant.
- A specialist health worker should be responsible for developing and adapting systems to facilitate access to services, to support and arrange care for those that cannot easily access services, and to liaise and work jointly with other agencies.

- Health promotion should be aimed at providing the means by which change can occur and at influencing authorities that can effect change.

- Local authority temporary accommodation should be in good repair, have adequate heating and ventilation, and be well supervised and maintained.

- Housing authorities should try to place families near to their former home to prevent disruption of schooling, family support, local support and health care.

- A specialist health worker and housing officer should perform a needs assessment prior to an offer of permanent housing being made.

CHAPTER 4

Child Mental Health Problems

Panos Vostanis

Mental health problems of homeless children

The previous chapter raised general health and developmental issues in pre-adolescent homeless children. The mental health of homeless children has been less systematically researched, and almost all the available data is based on research studies of children in homeless shelters in the USA (Bughra 1996). Various terms, such as behavioural problems/difficulties, psychosocial maladjustment or mental health disorders, are often used to describe the degree of deviance in children's psychological development.

In this text, the term *mental health problems* is used to refer to the broad range of *behavioural and emotional* difficulties which may cause concern or distress to a child, family, teacher or peers, and which can justify a clinical assessment with a view to treatment (Health Advisory Service 1995). When these problems become persistent and consistent, they constitute *mental health disorders*. Behavioural difficulties include aggression, hyperactivity and anti-social behaviour.

Emotional problems include anxiety, excessive fears, depression, self-harm behaviour, and separation anxiety. Other symptoms, such as eating problems, sleep disturbance, soiling and bed wetting, often occur together with behavioural and emotional difficulties. At any stage, about 20–25 per cent of children in the general population are estimated to present with mental health problems, particularly in areas of socio-economic adversity, and about 10–15 per cent with mental health disorders.

Previous studies in the USA have found high rates of behavioural and emotional problems among homeless children (Drennan and Stearn 1986; Heath 1994; Zima, Wells and Freeman 1994), with as many as 38 per cent of children having disorders of clinical significance (Fox *et al.* 1990). Problems such as sleep disturbance, eating problems, aggression and overactivity have been found among homeless children in two studies in the UK (Amery, Tomkins and Victor 1995; Conway 1988).

Mental health problems in childhood are often associated with developmental delays (these can be either cause or effect of learning/ developmental problems, or they could be both related to the same aetiological factors). A substantial proportion of homeless children have delayed development compared with the general population of children of similar age (Bassuk and Rosenberg 1990; Conway 1988; Fierman et al. 1991; Rescorla, Parker and Stolley 1991). This includes both specific developmental delays, such as in receptive and expressive language (Fox et al. 1990), visual, motor, and reading skills, as well as general educational attainment (Finkelstein and Parker 1993; Parker et al. 1991). Rafferty (1991) found that only 42 per cent of homeless children were reading at the level expected for their age.

Many of the health problems experienced by children in homeless families are common to children living in adversity (Masten et al. 1993). Nevertheless, American studies that compared homeless and low income families in housing found that children in the homeless families had significantly more developmental delays (Bassuk and Rosenberg 1988; Wood et al. 1990). Wood et al. found more behavioural problems, while Bassuk and Rosenberg identified higher levels of anxiety among children in homeless families. Mental health problems of single homeless teenagers and young adults are discussed in chapter five, as they constitute a different population with different needs from pre-school and pre-adolescent children.

Research into mental health problems among children has established an association with the presence of a number of risk factors, including physical or mental illness among parents, marital conflict and domestic violence (Rutter 1966; Rutter and Quinton 1984), and other stressors (Goodyer 1990; Pearce 1993). These include bereavement and other kinds of loss, accidents, house move or suspension from school. This means that children who are exposed to such adversities or life events are more vulnerable (or predisposed) to develop and maintain mental health problems. Risk factors usually have a cumulative effect, that is the degree of risk is associated to the number of adversities. They also interact with each other, for example, domestic violence and social instability may affect the mother's parenting capacity to nurture and discipline the child (see next chapter).

Risk factors are very common among homeless families, who are more likely than parents in samples of low income families to have experienced marital violence, mental illness, and drug and alcohol abuse, and less likely to have stable and supportive relationships (Bassuk and Rosenberg 1988; Bassuk et al. 1997; Wood et al. 1990). A high proportion of homeless mothers have psychiatric disorders (45% in Connelly and Crown 1994), particularly depression (Fox et al. 1990) and substance abuse (Parker et al. 1991). Histories of abuse have been widely reported both among homeless children and their mothers (Alperstein, Rappaport and Flanigan 1988; Bassuk et al. 1996). Poor social functioning and mental health disorders are particularly marked among homeless refugee families (Brooks and Patel 1995).

Specific risk factors have also been identified for family homelessness. Bassuk et al. (1997) found that children who had been placed in care or whose mothers used drugs were more likely to become homeless. Independent risk factors were also involved, such as recent eviction, being of ethnic minority status, family conflict and parent being admitted to hospital for a mental illness. There are also continuities between poverty, social and family adversities in childhood and homelessness in adult life (Koegel, Melamid and Burnam 1995).

A positive finding from research and clinical practice is that not all children exposed to risk factors will develop mental health problems. Resilience or protective factors have been uncovered and include: individual cognitive capacities; styles of acting rather than reacting; cognitive set or self-efficacy and problem solving; positive experiences of secure relationships, success and temperament; qualities which engender a positive response from others, and competency through overcoming stress successfully (Rutter 1985).

Although homelessness tends to disrupt relationships and supportive networks, and thus weaken these protective factors, the concept of children being able to cope with adversity has immense implications for intervention programmes with homeless children. One can hypothesise that if we break the cycle of adversity through a number of environmental, educational, social or health modalities, mental health problems can be contained or resolved, and secondary handicaps and disabilities can be prevented (Twaite and Lampert 1997). In other words, homeless children may be protected against the effect of risk factors by stability in other social relationships, such as with their wider family, their friends, or in school (Bassuk *et al.* 1997; Garmezy and Rutter 1983; Goodyer, Wright and Altham 1989).

There has been even less research on the long-term impact of homelessness on the family lives and mental health of children. For some families with multiple problems, homelessness may be an episode in a chaotic and unsettled life. Emotional and behavioural problems among their children may also be a chronic characteristic, which precedes homelessness, and which persists after rehousing. In other families, homelessness may precipitate a succession of adverse life events such as the disruption of family life and a severe deterioration in the domestic environment, with a consequent long-term impact on the mental health of the children involved. A third possibility is that for some families homelessness may be a brief episode from which they recover with only limited long-term impact on their children.

Mental health need established in the Birmingham study

The mothers

The majority of homeless mothers described a poor relationship with their partner, with domestic violence occurring in 41 families. The reverse pattern was established in housed families, with 18 mothers (or 90% of those who had a partner) describing their relationship as supportive and confiding. A high proportion of homeless mothers had scores on the General Health Questionnaire (GHQ) on or above the clinical threshold (49%), indicating a level of depression or distress of sufficient severity to require mental health treatment. This is similar to the rate among single homeless women found in a recent study at a London hostel (Adams *et al.* 1996), as well as other studies of homeless adults (Connelly and Crown 1994; Ferran, O'Shea and Davidson 1993; Zima *et al.* 1996).

These rates are about three times higher than among women of comparable age in the general population (Goldberg and Huxley 1992; Thompson *et al.* 1995), and much higher than in the comparison sample, in which none of the mothers had measurable psychiatric problems. Homeless mothers had significantly fewer attachment relationships, and lower social integration. The degree of mothers' mental health problems was best predicted by a history of previous abuse and previous number of accommodations. In other words, mental illness may reflect the underlying adverse life events that lead to homelessness.

The children

There were few differences in physical health and development between the children in the sample of homeless families and those in the comparison sample. Parents in the homeless sample reported that 28 per cent of the children had difficult births, 40 per cent had significant physical health problems, and 18 per cent had a developmental delay. These figures were similar to those for the children in the comparison sample. The average height and weight centiles for the children in both samples were within the normal range for the general population.

One distinctive feature of the homeless children was the score on the communication domain of the Vineland Adaptive Behaviour Scales. About 27 per cent had standard scores that were significantly below the norm expected for their age, compared with 18 per cent of children in the comparison group. This delay in communication distinguished the two samples, with homeless children having a level of communication significantly lower than that found among the children in the comparison sample.

Twenty-nine per cent of homeless children had total scores on the Child Behaviour Checklist (CBCL) above the clinical threshold, indicating the presence of mental health problems of sufficient severity to require referral for treatment (Table 4.1). These corresponded with the same proportion described by their parents as having behavioural problems.

Table 4.1 Children's reported problems

	Homeless (N=249)	Comparison (N=83)
History		
Established abuse (physical and/or sexual)	10%	0%
Previously in care	6%	1%
On at risk register	10%	0%
Significant mental health problems		
Above CBCL clinical cut-off ($p<0.05$)	29%	15%

Source: Vostanis et al. 1997

Forty-one per cent of homeless families had one or more children with CBCL scores above the clinical threshold. Mental health problems were much less common among children in the comparison sample. Fifteen per cent had total CBCL scores above the clinical threshold, and these tended to be concentrated in a small number (13 per cent) of families. The proportion of children in the comparison sample described by their parents as having a behavioural problem was 12 per cent, less than half the rate among homeless children. The impact of homelessness and the events that preceded it for many children can be illustrated by some of the reports given by children during interviews, a sample of which are included in Box 4.1.

Box 4.1 Impact on children's mental health

'My mum hit me when she found out. She beat my brother with a base-ball bat. I was sad and I cried, so did my brother'. (5 year old boy)

'I dream about it. I get pictures in my mind when I get into bed. Usually dad grabbing mum by the neck. I feel frightened and wish I could have done more for mum'. (8 year old girl)

Mental health problems among homeless children were frequently associated with other types of problems, particularly delayed communication skills and children's social dysfunction. However, the factors that best predicted children's mental health problems were mental health problems and social isolation among the mothers. The reverse pattern, that is mothers' mental health problems being predicted by children's behavioural/emotional difficulties, was not established. This suggests that help and treatment should be offered to both parents and children.

Mental health problems following rehousing

At one year follow-up, the proportion of homeless mothers who reported mental health problems of clinical significance (GHQ) had decreased from 49 per cent to 27 per cent, but still remained significantly higher than for comparison mothers at follow-up, or the general population. Because a substantial proportion of the original sample were lost to follow-up, we cannot generalise from this finding. However, it can be hypothesised that the remaining families were not in housing at the time, and may therefore have had a worse outcome in other psychosocial areas. Homeless mothers had more social support after rehousing, but were not socially integrated in their new locality (Interview Schedule for Social Interaction), particularly when compared with mothers in the comparison group. As in the original interview, lack of social support remained the factor that best predicted the continuation of mental health problems among mothers.

Eight children in the homeless sample had been placed on the child protection at risk register, and two had been in care since rehousing. Communication skills had improved since the first assessment but, overall, they were again significantly more likely to have low or moderately low scores on the communication domain of the Vineland Adaptive Behaviour Scales than comparison children at follow-up. One third (31%) of rehoused children had low or moderately low scores compared to 13 per cent of the comparison group.

Many children had mental health problems after rehousing. Mothers reported that 44 per cent of children had significant problems, and half (49.5%) had not improved since the family was rehoused. This view is supported by the children's scores on the Child Behaviour Checklist, which showed that 39 per cent had significant mental health problems (i.e. scores above the clinical threshold), compared to 11 per cent of the children in the comparison group.

The proportion of children in the homeless group who reached the clinical threshold had thus risen from 29 per cent at first interview to 39 per cent at follow-up. This is not an unexpected finding, bearing in mind the amount of disruption to home and school life that these children had faced, and the distress that this would have caused. The presence of mental health problems at the time of homelessness was the strongest predictor of similar problems after rehousing. In other words, children who presented with mental health problems when they became homeless were likely to continue to suffer from similar problems one year later. This indicates the importance of detection and intervention during children's stay at homeless centres as a means of preventing the development of chronic and severe disorders.

Implications for staff

Mechanisms of developing child mental health problems

Although there has been limited research into the needs of homeless children, previous findings from studies on social deprivation provide evidence that their mental health problems are affected by separation, loss, and dysfunctional family relationships (Bowlby 1980; Robins 1978; Rutter 1984). Family factors include physical or mental illness among parents (Rutter 1966), marital conflict, and domestic violence (Rutter and Quinton 1984).

In this study, almost half of the mothers had GHQ scores indicating the presence of mental health disorders, and 86 per cent of families had become homeless as a result of domestic or neighbourhood violence. These environmental factors have, however, been found to interact with child temperament (Thomas, Chess and Birch 1968) and predisposing biological factors, and this complex relationship is often believed to be the underlying mechanism that leads to the development of behavioural and emotional disorders in childhood and adolescence.

For families with multiple problems of this kind, homelessness may be one additional adverse life event (Goodyer 1990), or it may precipitate a succession of adverse life events, such as the disruption of family life and a severe deterioration in the domestic environment. As mentioned earlier, despite the adverse consequences of homelessness, not all children will be affected. In this study, one-third of homeless children had mental health problems of sufficient severity to require referral for treatment, at the time of homelessness and after rehousing. Even in adverse situations such as early institutional upbringing, it has been found that current life circumstances, such as quality of relationships, are as important as past experiences (Quinton and Rutter 1984). It is therefore essential to identify and sustain protective factors such as stability in school life and friendships (Goodyer, Wright and Altham 1989; Richman, Stevenson and Graham 1982; Robins 1970).

Assessment and detection of child mental health problems and disorders

Many professionals of varying backgrounds and disciplines (housing, education, social services, health or voluntary sector) have contact with homeless children and their families. As parents may not seek help for mental health problems at a period of turmoil and social breakdown, it is important that all staff have awareness of child mental health problems and can recognise them at a relatively early stage. For this reason, the principles of talking to children, particularly to establish emotional difficulties, are briefly summarised.

Our aim is to stress the general principles that apply to a variety of settings, rather than only to child mental health services. Even within the physical and time constraints of a busy hostel or school, a child should be preferably interviewed on his or her own. Children are often inhibited or frightened to answer questions on their emotional state in front of parents or known adults. Children as young as four to five years are aware of adults' emotions and views, and this can limit their account of their own thoughts and feelings.

Parents of pre-adolescents (i.e. younger than 12 years) should preferably be seen first, to give a more comprehensive history on their development and other related information. Adolescents may be more difficult to engage. In all cases, the young person should be reassured about the purpose of the interview. Family (joint) interviews are useful in establishing interaction of family members, as well as a means of initiating change in family relationships, but should not replace the initial individual contact with young people.

The current concerns or complaints (nature, context, duration) are explored first. Also, what kind of help or treatment has been previously received, and why the family may be seeking help at this particular time. For example, parents may not share teachers' concerns on the child's behaviour, but feel obliged to attend, and their lack of motivation to change will be counterproductive in future treatment. Not all of the following items of children's potential problems will need to be explored in depth. At the same time as eliciting information on symptoms or problems, the staff member can also assess parents' attitudes towards the child, the rest of the family and the described difficulties.

Important areas of children's functioning include: eating habits, somatic complaints (e.g. sickness, nausea, stomach aches, other kinds of pain), habits of elimination (soiling, wetting clothes at daytime, bed wetting), sleep pattern and habits, restlessness or overactivity, tics, speech, emotional state (depressive and anxiety symptoms), response to separation from main carer, attention and concentration, behaviour (accounts may be vague or critical of the child, particularly at the first assessment, for which reason it is useful to seek specific examples of reported behaviour: 'Could you give me an example of A being naughty? What happens when you ask him to go to bed? What does he actually do?')

The child's early development (motor skills, language, social functioning, toilet training, personal skills) and temperament (easy baby, placid, irritable, etc.) need to be explored, particularly the areas of parental concern. School history includes exploration of learning capacity and social functioning. History or presence of physical illness and of medical/nursing treatment could be relevant.

Homeless parents may be particularly sensitive to questions on family history of mental illness or family relationships. An introductory statement/explanation can put them at ease ('I would like to get a picture of A's life by asking a few questions about the family'). The child's social functioning and ability to make and maintain peer relationships is a good predictor of outcome, and is therefore a routine part of the assessment. Psychosexual and forensic history (offences, convictions) may be applicable to adolescents.

Engaging the child should be the priority at the start of the assessment interview. This is achieved by clarifying his or her understanding of the interview, explaining the assessment procedure, and alleviating any fears of stigma attached to mental illness or being seen by a mental health worker. Questions on hobbies, friends and interests enable an anxious child to relax, and to establish rapport with the interviewer. Some children will initiate a discussion on the presenting problems with very little prompting. Younger children often communicate through non-verbal means such as play and drawing.

What is important is that the interviewer remains sensitive and sympathetic, uses the child's clues or material in asking relevant questions, while remaining in control, and maintaining the structure and plan of the assessment interview. The child's perceptions of the family and school, as well as his or her self-perceptions are constantly being assessed. Important observations and information also include his or her appearance and behaviour during the interview, his or her ability to make rapport, and his or her attitude to future treatment.

The structure of the interview to assess a child's inner world depends on his or her age, particularly his or her cognitive development. Open and closed questions are asked on fears or anxieties (about themselves, parents, being homeless, past traumas or anticipation of the future) and related symptoms, mood and depressive symptoms, thoughts of self-harm, fears, obsessions, sleep (nightmares), eating, and perception of behavioural problems. Also, in relation to abnormal (psychotic) experiences, such as delusions and hallucinations, which are rare in this age group. Children's wishes and hopes for the future (in relation to housing, school or family) are very important.

Treatment and outcome of child mental health problems

Although the description of management and treatment of child mental health problems is beyond the remit of this chapter, it is important to acknowledge aspects relevant to homeless children and their parents. As children and families often present with a number of inter-related difficulties, management or treatment is multi-focused and not restricted to 'narrow' psychiatric interventions. This is essential for the development of services for homeless children and families. Another important principle is that initiation of treatment can have a rapid and significant impact on children's emotional well-being even during the period of crisis (homelessness in this case). Any treatment intervention should be adapted to the needs of these families, that is, via outreach clinics at the centres and work though the residential care staff. Such models are discussed in Chapter 9.

Psychological therapies include:

1. *Behavioural therapy,* which targets the symptoms without necessarily addressing underlying problems; for example, helping children or adults deal with panic attacks or specific fears (phobias), and parents deal with child behavioural problems.

2. *Brief psychodynamic psychotherapy,* which can enable the child to gain insight into the impact of the traumatic experience, for example witnessing domestic violence and developing nightmares and other post-traumatic stress symptoms.

3. *Cognitive therapy* targets negative patterns of thinking associated with depression. It can be particularly helpful for adolescents and parents, by helping them develop more adaptive ways of coping with the social and family breakdown.

4. *Family work* and *family therapy* aim to change family relationships. Although this is an ambitious target in most cases, family work and support can be initiated at the time of crisis.

As already mentioned, educational help (attendance, achievement, special needs provision, school-related behaviour programme) and social care (activities, advocacy, child protection) are integral parts of a treatment/ management plan. The treatment of concurrent physical health problems is also essential. Drug treatment may be indicated, for example in cases of severe parental depression or child attention deficit hyperactivity disorder, in combination with psychosocial approaches. Last, environmental changes may be necessary for child protection reasons (foster or residential care) or hospital admission for severe adolescent or parental mental illness.

Conclusions and recommendations

- Children and parents who become homeless constitute a high risk group for the development of mental health problems and disorders. These problems are often caused by life events and adversities that precipitate homelessness, but also by subsequent losses and the removal of protective factors. Their high level of need justifies the development of services that specifically target homeless families and their children.

- Although children's and parents' problems are inter-related, their individual mental health needs should be addressed, as they require different clinical skills of assessment and treatment.

- Treatment should be multi-focused, rather than merely psychiatric, i.e. it should target in parallel educational, emotional, behavioural, physical/developmental and social problems. Child and family mental health workers should preferably work within a designated primary care team.

- The characteristics of homeless children and families should be taken into account in the development of treatment programmes. For example, there should be co-ordinated action between health, housing, social services and education departments to exchange information on child protection and other risk factors at the time of admission to a homeless centre. This will help the early detection of problems by the staff and mental health workers. There is little point in referring children and parents to mainstream services with waiting lists, during their stay at homeless centres. The designated workers should refer families to local services after they have been rehoused.

- The role of staff working in homeless centres is essential in the success of such services. Mental health workers should work closely with residential staff and establish training programmes on mental health and related issues.

CHAPTER 5

Parenting Issues
in Homeless Families

Jacqueline Barnes

Homelessness, parenting and ecological theory

Homelessness is an example of a sociocultural risk with profound implications for parenting, with its lack of permanence and the absence of a place to be connected to and to identify with (Garbarino and Kostelny 1995). Since Baumrind's classic studies of the 1960s, parenting has been conceptualised as a combination of demandingness – the amount of control the parent attempts to exert over the child, and responsiveness – the extent to which the parent's behaviour addresses the needs and actions of the child. A parent who is both demanding and responsive is thought to be especially effective since this balance of attitudes has been shown to enhance child development while reducing parent–child conflict. One can easily think of ways in which the experience of homelessness might influence both of these dimensions of parenting.

This chapter examines the potential vulnerability of homeless families to parenting difficulties, using an ecological model. There is increasing acknowledgement of the ways in which the environment may influence family life and child development. The ecological model of child and family functioning (Bronfenbrenner 1979) has been the basis for understanding a wide range of family and parenting difficulties (Belsky 1980; Cicchetti and Lynch 1993; Garbarino and Kostelny 1992; Richters and Martinez 1993) and in the USA it was a key focus of the National Research Council's Panel on Research on Child Abuse and Neglect (1993). Sociologists have highlighted how structural and cultural dimensions of community social organisations are relevant to child development and family functioning (Brooks-Gunn *et al.* 1993; Furstenberg 1993; Sampson 1992; Wilson 1987).

Bronfenbrenner's (1979) multi-system ecological model for human development provides a theoretical framework for understanding the complexity of family life. His model recognises both the interdependent interaction of systems (mesosystems) and the importance of the social context. The immediate and possibly most powerful level, the microsystem of the family, is conceptualised within and interacting with institutional structures such as neighbourhood, school, workplace, and church, all placed in the exosystem. The exosystem in turn is conceptualised within the broader macrosystem of cultural context, which limits and shapes what occurs at the inner levels. Viewing family functioning from an ecological perspective allows all the influences affecting parent–child interactions to become visible concurrently. Actions to prevent parenting problems by reducing risk and reinforcing protective factors at each level, preferably in comprehensive and co-ordinated initiatives, can then be piloted, evaluated, and replicated.

Beyond the level of the family, aspects of the community which place families at risks for parenting problems include: lack of attachment of the family to the community; isolation from community networks and services; dislocation from services for children such as schools and health care; and the presence of danger and disorder in the neighbourhood (Sampson 1992). These factors may set resource constraints and generate stressors that affect the parent's capacity to care for her or himself and for others. Societies differ in the ways that temporary housing is provided for homeless families. In the USA shelters are often used by families with children (Bassuk, Rubin and Lauriat 1986), while in the UK more homeless families are placed in bed and breakfast hotels and other temporary placements by local housing authorities (Audit Commission Report 1989; Irvine 1996). In both systems, however, it is often the case that families will be living at some distance from their previous home. Two key aspects of their temporary accommodation may have a major impact on the extent to which a family is attached to their community or connected to relevant services: proximity (in terms of distance and transport) to existing social networks, both institutional (health care, education, social services) and informal (friends, child care); and the nature of the community in which they are placed.

Specific risk factors

Social isolation

From an ecological perspective, absence of social support and community level interactions are likely to influence parenting (Belsky 1984), with increased risk of child abuse (National Research Council 1993). For instance, it has been demonstrated in impoverished neighbourhoods in the USA that, over and above the difficulties of living in a neighbourhood with few resources for parents and children, social isolation is associated with higher levels of child maltreatment (Garbarino and Kostelny 1992). The sense of belonging, friendliness, and lack of alienation of community members is common to many theoretical approaches to what constitutes a psychological sense of community (McMillan and Chavis 1986; Puddifoot 1996). Thus, social isolation may be one of the major risk factors for parenting problems, but one which has the potential for amelioration with changes in housing policy and improvements in support networks.

Homelessness places families in situations where, in order to gain shelter, they may lose existing social support and status within institutional systems such as education and health (Hausman and Hammen 1993; Milburn and D' Ercole 1991). In the USA, it was found that lack of social support was a crucial difference between homeless mothers and their housed low income counterparts (Bassuk and Rosenberg 1988). In London, as many as 60 to 70 per cent of families with children are placed outside the local authority area responsible for accepting them as officially homeless and providing them with accommodation (Royal College of Physicians 1994). Housing authorities take many factors into account and may place families at locations some distance from their existing home in order to provide housing in street properties rather than hostels, in an environment that offers ethnic or religious institutions, agencies such as housing associations, community centres, or day centres of centrally located shopping facilities. The key aspect of placement in a different area for families with children is geographical displacement – moving from one school's catchment area to another, from one local education authority to another, moving away from a general practitioner, placement on the wrong' side of a major barrier such as a river or major road. All these can have a significant impact on family life.

Placements of families in neighbourhoods where they have no connections or local knowledge can engender psychological homelessness characterised by a sense of isolation and lack of attachment to the community (Gill 1992), which contributes to families feeling powerless (Victor, Jefferies and Barrett 1990). Children are frequently on waiting lists before they can obtain placements in local schools (HM Inspectorate of Schools 1990), their education is disrupted by problems with transfer of records and other essential information (Power, Whitty and Youdell 1995), and disruption from registration with a general practitioner leads to reliance on hospital accident and emergency departments (Lissauer et al. 1993).

Nature of the community

While all efforts are made by housing authorities to find suitable homes, homeless families with young children may be placed in communities where others are unwilling to be housed, due to community problems. Social disorganisation of communities is characterised by absence of social networks among neighbours, observable social disorder, racial cleavages and a subculture of violence. It has been linked with a number of developmental outcomes including substance abuse and delinquency (Sampson and Groves 1989; Simcha-Fagan and Schwartz 1986), child abuse (Earls, McGuire and Shay 1994; Garbarino and Kostelny 1992; National Research Council 1993), teenage pregnancy (Brooks-Gunn et al. 1993) and academic attainment (Duncan, Brooks-Gunn and Klebanov 1994).

Families in socially disorganised communities with limited neighbourhood control are more isolated in their family management practices, and more vulnerable to problems such as child abuse and neglect, whereas parents in socially organised communities, especially mothers, are more likely to be linked into social support networks that reinforce positive child rearing practices (Furstenberg 1993). There is evidence for the influence of social disorder and limited social networks on rates of child abuse and neglect (Garbarino and Kostelny 1992), particularly where there is high population turnover, a large number of single parents, and a high proportion of children to adults (Coulton 1995) and evidence of housing decay (Zuravin and Taylor 1987). Placement of homeless families in these kinds of communities will neither further the interests of the community, nor enable the homeless families to be competent in their parenting.

Parent and child characteristics

The health of homeless people may be poor before they become homeless, and may also be influenced by problems with access to health care services. Homeless parents have more chronic health problems (Patterson and Roderick 1990; Victor 1992). As summarised in Chapter 2, child health problems identified in homeless children include poor diet (Stitt, Griffiths and Grant 1994), low birth weight and general poor health (Parsons 1991). In Oxford, almost half of a sample of homeless parents reported that their children's health had deteriorated since moving into bed and breakfast accommodation (Vickers 1991). Homeless families are less likely than the general population to be registered with a general practitioner, which reduces their chances of primary and secondary health care, as well as preventive services such as immunisations (Royal College of Physicians 1994). As a consequence, they rely on accident and emergency departments for medical treatment (Lissauer *et al.* 1993). One London study found that ten per cent of paediatric beds were occupied by children from homeless families (Victor *et al.* 1989).

Parents who are homeless are likely to have mental health difficulties, although not to the extent of the single homeless, and these are not necessarily the cause of their homeless state (Bassuk and Rosenberg 1988; Smith and North 1994). In the USA, homeless mothers have more psychiatric problems than neighbourhood controls (Buckner, Bassuk and Zima 1993). Evidence from the UK is equivocal because studies of hostel residents have not separated single homeless adults from parents with families. In Sheffield, three-quarters of adult hostel residents were found to be at risk of major depressive illness (Usherwood, Jones and Hanover Project Team 1993). In North West Thames, compared with 18 per cent of local residents, almost half (45%) of the homeless population had significant mental morbidity (Victor 1992).

As described in Chapter 4, almost half the mothers in two studies of women living in a Birmingham hostel for homeless families were identified as having psychiatric morbidity (Vostanis *et al.* 1996, 1997), a much higher rate than is found in the general population. Whether the parental mental health problems are long-standing or recent, the family will be at greater risk if they are socially isolated, since lack of social support is a significant contributor to depression in women with children (Brown and Harris 1978).

Children in homeless families, as reported in other contributions to this volume, also experience higher levels of emotional and behavioural problems than low SES controls (Rescorla, Parker and Stolley 1991; Schteingart *et al.* 1995; Vostanis *et al.* 1996, 1997; Ziesemer, Marcoux and Marwell, 1994). Homeless children have particular difficulties in maintaining social relationships and keeping up with academic activities (Masten *et al.* 1993; Power, Whitty and Youdell 1995).

Impact on family functioning

Homelessness may place many demands on families. Even the most skilled parent is likely to be challenged by the competing demands of gaining adequate accommodation and maintaining continuity in their children's lives (Hausman and Hammen 1993). Not only may the disruptions have an impact on the physical and mental health of both children and parents, but many factors associated with homelessness may impair a parent's capacity to provide protection and support. While the stresses of homelessness may be similar to those associated with living in poverty, families who are homeless typically experience multiple risks and are therefore especially vulnerable (Rutter 1981). However, the particular burden that homelessness places on parenting and the ways in which parents and children cope with specific risks have not been thoroughly investigated.

There have been no systematic studies of how homeless families in the UK cope with the day-to-day effects of their family's social isolation and lack of institutional and informal networks, often in the context of socially disorganised communities. Anecdotal reports from health visitors suggest that many homeless families are finding it difficult to cope. Mothers in an Oxford survey reported that they felt tired most of the time (68%), that they were unhappy (60%), that they could not sleep at night (58%), often lost their temper (65%), and were irritated with their child (55%) (Vickers 1991). Reports collected by professionals working with homeless families in the USA indicate that, while most of the mothers cared deeply about being 'good parents', the immediate demands of finding food and shelter precluded them from focusing on their children's, health and development for instance by ensuring school enrolment, registering with health care services (Hausman and Hammen 1993). Deleterious effects were noted in some women's reliance on children for company, and on their use of older children (often only aged five or six years) to care for younger family members.

Extrapolations can be made from studies concerned with the importance of housing as a factor in the socialisation of children. Bartlett (1997) reviews this topic, highlighting the way in which the family's ability to shape their own home environment reflects the way in which they can create opportunities for their children and communicate norms and expectations. The symbolic importance of the home as a place to demonstrate one's beliefs and values to children has been highlighted (Sebba and Churchman 1986). Sociologists have argued that, once the basic needs of housing and shelter have been met, the home has other functions related to self-expression

(Rainwater 1966). Bartlett (1997) concludes that in situations such as homelessness, when housing limits parents' capacities to exercise control through the organisation of the home environment, there are likely to be difficulties in raising children.

Type of housing, overcrowding, access to outdoors, noise level, and the characteristics of close neighbours are all likely to have an impact on parents' efforts to discipline and monitor their children. A study in Switzerland demonstrated that the quality of parent–child relationships between five years olds and their parents were influenced by traffic levels, with more anxiety and less flexible child-rearing strategies used in areas perceived to have dangerous traffic (Huttenmoser 1995). A number of studies in the UK and the USA have related crowded household conditions to punitive parenting (Newson and Newson 1965; Peterman 1981). Even in circumstances where social support is available, it has been found that crowded conditions have an impact on the quality of parental behaviour (Wachs and Camli 1991). Thus one can imagine how the circumstances of homeless families, living in temporary accommodation which they have not chosen for themselves, which is usually overcrowded and may not provide outdoor play space for their children, may influence parenting.

It must be emphasised, however, that notwithstanding all the difficulties they face, many homeless mothers demonstrate significant strengths and coping strategies, sacrificing for their children, struggling with limitations, guarding their children from harm and seeking solutions to their difficulties (Hodnicki and Horner 1993; Montgomery 1994; Smith and North 1994). It has been suggested that developing personal meaning in relation to adversity is an effective way of coping (Beardslee 1989). Information from the lives of homeless women and children who are demonstrating resilience in the face of multiple difficulties may be useful in helping policy makers to develop appropriate resources and to provide support for less resilient families.

Some illustrative cases

The comments of families from a small qualitative pilot study in one London bed and breakfast hotel providing accommodation for homeless families illustrate some of the parenting issues that have been reviewed above, and indicate some topics that need to be investigated in more detail, so that suitable support can be provided for parenting in homeless families. The hotel, comprising a row of large four-storey Victorian houses, was located in a central London borough. The families placed there came, however, from a neighbouring local authority. Families were contacted through the local health visitor, by meeting those using a drop-in play service within the hotel, and by meeting families using another local drop-in centre that had a laundry and provided meals and a toy library among other services. The aim of the study was to locate families with children aged between 2 and 12 years of age to explore parenting issues in relation to homelessness. Using semi-structured interviews, the families were asked about how they came to be homeless, about their own physical and mental health and that of their children, and the extent of child behaviour problems. In relation to parenting, they were asked about their home routine including potentially positive aspects of parenting, such as shared leisure time activities, reading, playing or cooking together and about specific discipline issues that had arisen in the past few weeks. They were also asked to think how the experience of homelessness had influenced their family. The interviews were tape-recorded and transcribed. Several themes emerged from the interviews.

Social isolation and its relevance to maternal mental health

Several of the women interviewed reported current depressive symptoms. It was clear that the social isolation, which was typical of their circumstances, exacerbated their depression. A young woman who had experienced repeated depressive episodes, including a suicide attempt in her teens, and who was currently receiving medication for depression, said: 'Sometimes I just sit here, and if I have pains I don't go up the street. I just sit here. It's no life for me and them (the children)'.

This young woman, who described a number of violent and traumatic episodes in her past, was able to summon sufficient energy to get her daughter to school and from school. However, her current living circumstances, isolated from previous neighbours and with all her family abroad, provided few resources if she needed help with her children. Asked if there was anyone in the hotel, or locally, who would help her out with the care of her two year old, she said: 'I haven't got no one. I am very exhausted. I haven't had a break since he was born'.

Asked how many adults she knew in the neighbourhood, she also reported keeping herself to herself: 'I don't want to mix so I just say "Hello", "Goodbye" that's it, finished. I haven't got around to talking, everybody is in their room. I don't go down to the dining room, because I've got my own television. I don't even go down for breakfast. I just keep to myself here'.

The way in which the situation of homelessness contributed to social isolation was also noted by another mother, albeit one who was currently able to maintain a well-organised family life for her three children: 'I feel for me socially, it has an effect because I can't invite people here whereas before, I liked to cook, I liked to invite friends around, so I feel in that respect being cut off from part of life, losing contact with people that I had more contact with before'.

Dislocation from appropriate services can also seriously influence family life and increase pressure on parents already under stress. One mother of four, a refugee who described ongoing depressive symptoms related to the loss of contact with her extended family, had a 12-year-old son with a serious hearing disability. He could not gain a place in a special school until the family knew where the housing authority was going to place them. While waiting, he was home all day and had been subject to bullying by other children when he went to the TV lounge or the garden of the hotel. His mother described his experiences: 'He is always here, he doesn't go to school so he has nothing to do. I teach him for two hours and we play games together, and the rest of the day he just sits there. They think that because he can't hear them then he cannot communicate with me, but he comes up and tells me'.

Parent–child conflicts related to overcrowding and lack of space to play

While isolated from previous friends and neighbours, or family members, there is often unwelcome proximity to other families in temporary accommodation such as bed and breakfast hotels, which can only be avoided by staying within the confines of their private rooms. This may place family members in situations that lead to conflict. As one mother said: 'Having no privacy is one of the worst things, never having any privacy, and never having any space, eating here and sleeping here and working all together it just feels unhygienic'.

The close proximity is likely to have an effect on the amount of child-related stress that a parent can tolerate. As this mother of three (aged three, seven and nine years) noted: 'I have become more impatient with them. I can't go in another room. We are all together here, and if they are here shouting or screaming or they want to watch something on TV, I am having to sit through whatever they do. We have to do it all together'. This was a common theme for parents. A mother of four (aged one, seven, eight and twelve years) said: 'They get on my nerves because they don't know what to do, and they play for a little, and there is nothing more to do, and what can I do for them … it's like being put in a prison here'.

The lack of space means that older children often have to complete their school work with younger siblings close at hand, which may precipitate conflict that needs to be managed. One mother explained why she had shouted at her daughter: 'It was about him. I wanted her (aged 11 years) to give him (aged two years) a pen, to share. She started shouting at me and she said "No". I don't know if it's being in one room, she can't do her homework, he's bugging her and all that. I just said "Why don't you just give it to him?" and she said "No"… and I said "I am your mother you know" and she was angry with me'.

Several other families also described problems with older children not wanting to share pens, or having them grabbed by toddlers when the school aged children were doing homework. In general, the constant need to tidy in a confined space and the inability to give older children some private space created discipline situations for most of the families interviewed.

Safety concerns and interaction with other residents

Many families were wary of allowing their children to wander in the common areas of the building, expressing concerns about other residents, although they are also aware of the need that their children had for exercise and new surroundings. A father of a three-year-old girl remarked: 'She likes to play, she likes to run out, but I don't want her to go out, to play with these kids. She is happy when I take her outside or to Hyde Park. I don't like her to go out of this room, because someone might do something bad to her. She wants to go out. She doesn't like to stay in the room'.

The mother of four, mentioned above, had similar reservations about letting older children go to the common areas, such as the television lounge. Describing a dispute in the past week with her eight-year-old daughter, the mother said: 'She wants to go down in the TV room, but there are children I don't want her to have contact with, because one of them, well two of them, a sister and brother, they bully her. But there is nowhere to go. They have to stay in this room, they have to sleep here, to eat here, to play here, and she gets fed up, because it's difficult for a child to be home from school and then in this room; so she likes to watch TV, but she got bullied by these children, then she came up here crying'.

In another family their eldest child, a ten-year-old boy, had been in a fight with some children in the communal garden and one of the other mothers hit him, so now he was not permitted to play outside, a continuing source of discord between him and his parents. The management of the hotel had been fairly supportive, but were threatening to deny all the children any access to the garden without the presence of a parent, which would pose many more problems for families such as this one with several younger siblings, including an infant.

Resilience and positive attributions

Notwithstanding the many difficulties encountered in bed and breakfast accommodation, some of those parents interviewed were able to gain some strength from their experience. One mother noted how it had drawn the family together. She remarked: 'It has put a lot of pressure on the relationship with my husband but as I say in the same way it's also some sort of positive effect in that it's maybe brought us closer together in some way that we are struggling together, managing to face the problems together. It's a very close family. We are very close. Whether that (living in one room) made us close or not ... but maybe it has'.

Another family found that the bed and breakfast gave them more autonomy than they had experienced when living in a friend's house. The father, on being asked what living in the hostel meant to them, said: 'She (his wife, who was not English speaking) is all right now, because before she couldn't do anything because she was staying with a friend, she wants to cook and she can't, she wants to change the baby and she can't. But now she can and now we feel that is our place'.

Coping in circumstances that are less than optimal for family life can sometimes provide parents with a sense of worth by their ability to move their children away from more serious risks such as family violence or racial abuse. The mother who described depression was, nevertheless, able to compare her current neighbourhood favourably with her previous housing, in a suburban estate with a great deal of violence and racial trouble. Even more optimistically, another mother was able to see the importance of being in transition and in the mean time was hopeful that she could benefit from the more economical lifestyle. Asked what advice she would give to other families in her circumstances, she said: 'If they were having to go through being homeless, I would say just keep positive, just to think that hopefully at the end of the day it's going to be worthwhile, and you are going to be settled, you know, just to make the best of it and look at the positive aspects, that it's obviously cheaper, you may have a chance even to save a little money

... there is a nominal charge when you are on benefits, no phone bills, no water bills, nothing at all, you don't have to worry about the roof falling down and you paying for it, so in that respect it can be quite good, you can save some money'.

Few parents may be able to sustain this level of optimism in the face of overcrowded living conditions and ongoing disputes between the children, but her use of positive attributions provides some ways that families can be helped to reframe their circumstances, so that, within their own personal stories, they can develop coping skills.

Conclusions and recommendations

This review of the literature, complemented by comments from families, shows how important it is to offer homeless families support with parenting. There are also some key points for authorities responsible for making housing decisions. There are several specific areas of concern:

- Housing placement can lead to social isolation from support networks. Several successful parenting initiatives have demonstrated how helpful informal social networks can be in preventing difficulties such as maternal depression (Pound and Mills 1985) and child abuse (Olds et al. 1986). While every effort should be made to keep families within the communities where they have been living, for those who are refugees or who have to move, perhaps to escape violence, attention should be given to helping them reestablish networks.

- There is a growing amount of evidence demonstrating which community characteristics help to promote social networks for families who are isolated (Barnes-McGuire 1997) and how to measure them (Barnes 1997). While it may be necessary for housing departments to place a family at a distance from existing networks, some community contexts may be more supportive than others and the extent of community cohesion should be part of housing policy procedures. The institutional links with education, health and social services also need to be a high priority, when families are moved.

- Some families are particularly vulnerable to the impact of social isolation. It is not clear from current research which families are the most vulnerable, is it those with infants, school-age children, teenagers, children with special educational needs, or children with serious medical conditions? Does family structure make a difference? Future research should address these topics, and will need to clarify what support services are needed. Drop-in centres have been piloted (Hammond and Bell 1995), which give family support and advice with parenting problems. Centres such as this could provide a focal point where families can link up with local facilities, and also gain some immediate respite in terms of child care, playgroup, or after-school activities, which would benefit most families. Centres could, in addition, bring together families who are using a range of coping strategies, and in this way their resilience may help to shape additional services designed to help homeless families.

In the UK, single homeless people have benefited from the chance to earn by selling the *Big Issue*, a magazine that is only available on the street from ID carrying adults who are all homeless. They keep the profit from each copy sold and any extra money that purchasers decide to give them. It enables them to move away from begging to feel less stigmatised, and has given many single homeless individuals a sense of achievement and self-worth. They also form social networks with other homeless people at the magazine's distribution centres, but this is not very practical for a parent with children to care for. Many parents and children are also demonstrating resourcefulness and creativity in coping and their experiences should be a source of strength to many other families facing similar circumstances.

CHAPTER 6

Homeless Children
and Domestic Violence

Gill Hague and Ellen Malos

Introduction

Domestic violence is currently in public view in an historically unprecedented way. Defined here to mean violence against women by men with whom they have, or have previously had, an intimate relationship, it features now in arenas as disparate as government policy and *The Archers* or *Eastenders*. Refuges and other emergency services are an established feature of social provision, the police response has been subject to some improvements, many agencies have developed practice guidelines and domestic violence training, and both multi-agency and public education initiatives are multiplying (ACOP 1996; Grace 1995; Hague and Malos 1998; Harwin, Malos and Hague 1998; Home Office 1990; Mullender 1996).

Nevertheless, domestic violence shows no signs of abating and is in fact shockingly common, featuring in between one in ten and one in four male / female relationships in Britain (Department of Health 1997; Mooney 1994; Stanko *et al.* 1998). At a global level, the deleterious effects of domestic violence are increasingly recognised on world agendas, for example, in the historic 1993 *United Nations Declaration on the Elimination of Violence against Women* and the *Global Platform for Action* adopted by countries around the world as a result of the 1995 World Conference of Women in Beijing (United Nations 1995). Within this gathering interest, the plight of children witnessing, living with or otherwise experiencing domestic violence has not passed unnoticed in recent years, particularly in the USA, the UK and Canada. The impact on children of domestic violence has become an issue which has 'found its time' (see for example Mullender 1996; Mullender and Morley 1994).

We now know that children respond in a variety of different ways to violence in the home and many demonstrate admirable coping strategies. However, almost all are affected in some ways. Children may become more withdrawn or more aggressive, not necessarily along stereotyped gender lines. They may experience high levels of fear and anxiety, and have problems in school and in relationships. The impacts of living with domestic violence are complex and not necessarily permanent, but many children do carry long-term effects into adulthood. Both domestic violence and child abuse occur in many families, and some new initiatives in child protection work in relation to domestic violence have now been put into effect in both the UK and other countries. It is beginning to be understood that experiencing domestic violence (between adults) is abusive to children in itself (see Hague, Malos and Dear 1996; Mullender and Morley 1994).

Despite the new attention to the issue of domestic violence overall, however, services in the UK are still inadequate and piecemeal. It will be argued in this chapter that housing policy in particular fails to meet the needs of abused women and their children.

Homelessness and freedom from violence

There are many great injustices associated with domestic violence. One of them is that, if women are abused, it is normally their children and themselves who also lose their homes, support networks and communities. In the pursuit of safety, many thousands of women and children face homelessness in this country annually, while their abusers remain at home.

On a general level, various domestic violence projects around the world are attempting to develop multi-faceted, inter-agency community intervention projects, which include a strong criminal justice and community response. The best known is probably the Duluth Domestic Abuse Intervention Project in Minnesota, USA (see for example Pence 1988) although similar projects exist in Minneapolis, Seattle, Quincy in Massachusetts and elsewhere. One of the long-term goals of projects of this type is to enable abused women and their children to stay safely in their own homes. In aiming so high, they are building towards a future in which domestic violence is no longer tolerated by communities and by society, but this admirable outcome is as yet a long way down the line.

Meanwhile, women experiencing violence and their children are forced on a daily basis to leave home, often at very short notice, to hide in refuges, to live for months or even years in temporary accommodation and to lose their homes and everything they previously owned. Domestic violence is one of the main causes of child homelessness affecting many thousands of children annually.

The Domestic Violence Research Group at the University of Bristol conducts national and international studies of domestic violence and offers consultancy, teaching and training on the issue. This chapter draws on a two year national research study into local authority housing responses to domestic violence by a team within the group, supported by the Joseph Rowntree Foundation (Malos and Hague 1993). Recent consultations with practitioners in the domestic violence, refuge and housing fields indicate that the findings of this study still stand and that the situation of women and children homeless due to violence has in fact worsened since the research was undertaken.

The need for temporary and permanent housing

It has been well-documented in Europe, North America and elsewhere that one of the most urgent and important needs of abused women and their children is for somewhere safe to go: in other words for supportive emergency accommodation, followed by access to permanent housing options of a decent standard which offer security and safety (see for example Dobash and Dobash 1992). Our UK study specifically demonstrated the continuing importance of access to local authority and social rented housing (Malos and Hague 1993 and 1997) but also documented increasing difficulties for abused women and children in accessing this housing.

In countries like the USA where public housing is more stigmatised and less available, women and children may experience even greater difficulties in finding safe accommodation than they do in Britain, although rented accommodation is more readily obtainable. A stronger police response is of some help, and mandatory arrest policies for perpetrators are routinely operated in many provinces in Canada and states within the USA. Some specific children's projects have developed in both countries (e.g. the Women's Community House Children's Programme in London, Ontario) for children homeless due to domestic violence (Loosley 1994). However, stays in emergency shelters are often much shorter than in the UK, where families who have been accepted for permanent rehousing in social housing may wait for long periods until their accommodation becomes available.

The UK situation: refuges and the Women's Aid Federations

More than 300 refuges offering temporary accommodation to women and children homeless due to domestic violence now exist in the UK and these include specialist projects for black and minority ethnic women and children. Most commonly, these comprise Asian women's refuges, but African, Caribbean, Latin American, Turkish, Irish and Jewish specialist refuge projects also exist. The majority of refuges are affiliated to the national Women's Aid federations in Wales, Scotland, Northern Ireland and England which are the key national agencies representing abused women and their children. The federations monitor legislation, policy and practice, and provide information, resources, training and networking. The amount of domestic violence which they document and deal with is depressingly large. Over 60,000 women and children are accommodated by Women's Aid in England alone each year, and a further 100,000 contact the English federation for advice and support. Thousands more contact the police and other agencies.

The Women's Aid federations, together with other women's organisations in the movement against domestic violence, deriving from the wider women's liberation movement of the 1970s, have now been campaigning against domestic violence and publicising the issue for 25 years (Dobash and Dobash 1992; Hague and Malos 1998). Their successes have been many, not least the establishment of the refuge network. However, there is still less than one-third of the refuge provision recommended back in 1975 by the *Select Committee on Violence in Marriage* (Parliamentary Select Committee 1975). Specialist refuges for women and children from minority ethnic communities are frequently even more severely under-resourced than general refuges in the same locality (Mama 1996). Overall, almost all existing services are hard-pressed to survive, facing recurrent funding crises and dependent on the good will of dedicated and usually over-worked staff. A worrying recent development has been the setting up of refuges with minimal staffing levels by many housing associations, without liaison with Women's Aid. These new refuges provide for the emergency housing needs of the women and children using their services, but usually do not cater for their social care needs.

Effects on children of homelessness

The disastrous impact on children of being homeless and of living for long periods in various types of temporary accommodation are discussed in detail in other parts of this book and have been well-documented (see for example, Malos 1993). They include negative effects on schooling, academic achievement, behaviour, and physical and mental health (see for example Conway 1988; Department of Education and Science HMI 1989; Evans 1991; Miller 1990; Rafferty 1991; Vostanis et al. 1997). Children in this situation lose their home, their friends, all their possessions and sometimes their family and relatives. They lose their school or playgroup, their security, their pets, their social circle. In other words, the very fabric of their lives can be destroyed by the homeless experience. However, while local authorities are required to provide preventative services to assist children in need under the Children Act (Department of Health 1989), many do not include homeless children in this category (see for example Tunstill and Aldgate 1994).

Impact of domestic violence on homelessness

When children have to leave home due to domestic violence, these circumstances add specific difficulties to the extremely traumatic nature of the homeless experience in general. In addition to all the other major losses noted above, children usually lose their family life and daily access to their fathers. Becoming homeless may happen for them very quickly, often in the middle of the night, with little or no warning whatsoever, and frequently as a result of a highly distressing incidence of violence between their parents, so that extreme shock, fear and sometimes terror are added to the experience.

Once they have left, both women and children describe living in constant fear and anxiety that they will be found and that the violence will begin again (Malos and Hague 1997). Often, children in this situation are literally in hiding and may be experiencing situations of profound personal trauma. In addition, the lack of security in most emergency housing – and in private rented options most particularly – is a severe hazard and one that can lead to the further abuse of both children and their mothers.

In our study, many women reported that their children's health or mental well-being had been seriously affected by the violence which they had experienced or witnessed, and being without a home had then compounded their difficulties. These mothers often felt helpless and desperate as their children became more and more disturbed by prolonged homelessness (Hague and Malos 1994a). In addition, women and children escaping violence are frequently forced to move to an unknown area where they know absolutely no one, have no support networks and may well not know where to turn for advocacy and help.

Many women and children escaping violence in the home make use of refuges rather than other types of temporary accommodation, as noted. Some of the worst aspects of poor temporary housing may therefore be avoided as, at their best, refuges provide a supportive environment, safe and secure, in which women and children are provided with counselling, advocacy, and support. Working with children is a priority for Women's Aid, and many refuges have children's workers on the staff and innovatory programmes of support work for children in operation. A recent cross-institutional study of children's work in refuges, which included the present authors, highlighted the creative approaches which this work often embraces, but also found that the main issue constantly holding back its development was severe lack of resources (Hague *et al.* 1996). Playrooms may only be open once a week, for instance, and child worker posts may have insecure or no funding. Children whom we interviewed for this 1996 study described the lack of facilities graphically, as they tried to make a go of their lives in overcrowded (although supportive) refuges (see for example Hague *et al.* 1996, pp. 81–101).

Attempts to get assistance from local authorities under the children in need provisions of the 1989 Children Act (Department of Health 1989) have been successful in some instances with grants for child work being made to a few refuges. However, the total of local authority funding for children's work in refuges throughout the UK is less than that obtained from the *BBC Children In Need Appeal* (Ball 1994; Hague *et al.* 1996).

While many children enjoy their stays in refuges, substantial difficulties were experienced in our study, sometimes due to the lack of any private space. The effects of disrupted schooling due to moving from refuge to refuge in the search for safety and the trauma of being homeless due to violence were often severe, despite the supportive atmosphere provided (Hague *et al.* 1996)

The Family Law Act 1996

Many women and children made homeless as a result of violence make use of the 1996 Family Law Act. Implemented in September 1997 (Lord Chancellor's Department 1996), Part IV of this Act improves the civil law remedies available. For example, orders are available under the Act to exclude the perpetrator of the violence from the home for periods of six months (or longer in some circumstances). The legislation also amends the 1989 Children Act (Department of Health 1989) to introduce a measure to exclude perpetrators of child abuse from the home. The new 1997 Prevention of Harassment Act (Lord Chancellor's Department 1997) may also be of some assistance, although we do not yet have any measures of its effectiveness. However, the usefulness of short-term legal remedies of this nature is limited in practice. A 1990 study of the effectiveness of the protection offered by the domestic violence legislation of the time, for example, was tellingly entitled *Not Worth the Paper* (Barron 1990). For those who have taken the momentous step of becoming homeless and living in temporary accommodation, taking out an order under the Family Law Act (Lord Chancellors Department 1996), and going back home again may be tantamount to courting disaster. In addition, courts cannot and will not issue orders banning a violent man from the family home permanently.

Many women and children made homeless due to violence know that, no matter how much they may want legal remedies to work and how much they may long to return home, it will never be safe to do so. There is much evidence that the most dangerous time for a woman experiencing domestic violence is just after she has left (Mirrlees-Black 1995). Perpetrators may go to enormous lengths to track down their partners and there have been numerous tragic instances of further abuse and violence if they are found. Women's Aid has documented various highly distressing cases where women have been killed in front of their children in or near refuges. Any consideration of the effects of the homelessness legislation on children and women escaping violence must be set against this very real background of danger, violence threat and, in extreme cases, death (WAFE 1994).

Previous homelessness legislation and domestic violence

Women's lesser access, compared with men, to better paid work and to financial resources generally (especially when they have children) has been firmly established. While some families who are homeless due to domestic violence will be able to make use of the private housing market, either as owners or as tenants, many are not in this financial position and are, therefore, disproportionately dependent on social housing provision as previously noted (Gilroy and Woods 1994; Muir and Ross 1993). Thus, if a safe return to their previous accommodation is not possible, access to a secure and affordable permanent home is vitally important and, despite the increasing problems which it faces, the public housing sector has remained a vital, if diminishing, resource for women and children escaping violence.

The duties contained within the 1977 Housing (Homeless Persons) Act (Department of the Environment 1977) and the later consolidated 1985 Housing Act (Department of Environment 1985) in regard to access to permanent rehousing were of considerable help to abused women and their children, although the effectiveness of these Acts was always somewhat unreliable due to the degree of discretion permitted (Binney, Harkell and Nixon 1985; Bull 1993; Charles 1993). However, the inclusion of domestic violence as an accepted cause of statutory homelessness was an early victory for the Women's Aid federations and other women's organisations (Hague and Malos 1994b). Thus, from the first, families escaping domestic violence formed one of the main groups of the statutorily homeless under the Act. DoE Housing statistics and many studies have found a figure for domestic violence cases of at least 15 per cent of homelessness acceptances (Bull 1993; Malos and Hague 1997). A recent research study found that 85 per cent of homeless families were escaping violence of one sort or another including neighbour and family violence, as well as partner abuse (Vostanis *et al.* 1997).

The previous homelessness legislation was limited by its own complexity in regard, for example, to the priority need, intentional homelessness and local connections provisions, and also the requirements for investigation and discretion – which were introduced because of fears of the law becoming an easy road into local authority tenancies when it was passed in 1977 (Department of Environment 1994). Since then, in addition, the government has substantially reduced the availability of public rented housing, through its policy of changing the role of local housing authorities from that of provider to that of enabler, put into practice by cuts in public housing finance, by the right to buy and by the transfer of the provider role to housing associations and private housing companies. Together these measures have meant that homeless households have frequently experienced greater and greater housing difficulty.

While some families in our study were rehoused in a matter of months, or even, exceptionally, weeks, many waited for very long periods in temporary accommodation with detrimental effects on the children. Contrary to the government suggestions which fuelled the 1996 Housing Act (Department of Environment 1996), our research showed no evidence that these groups received unfair 'fast track' precedence (see Department of Environment 1994; Welsh Women's Aid 1994). Rather, the queues of women and children waiting for rehousing were lengthening as an effect of the cut-back in public housing in many areas. There was little evidence that housing associations were making up for the shortfall although they did make a valuable contribution which has increased substantially since the research was conducted.

Often, abused women also face a greater uncertainty than some other applicants about whether the local authority will accept them for temporary rehousing because of the difficulty of proving the violence, despite improvements made by many authorities in recent years in their policies of listening to abused women's stories. Difficulties of belief and proof apply especially if women applicants have suffered psychological or sexual, rather than physical, violence.

In our own study, there was much variation in the way in which families were treated during their applications. On one end of the spectrum were authorities where women and children applicants were treated with respect, where a believing attitude was adopted, and where attempts were made to rehouse quickly and to meet applicants' needs. At the other pole were authorities who were obstructive at every turn, a response which was not always explicable in terms of the amount of housing stock which the authority controlled.

Hold-ups and uncertainties

Various women in our study faced protracted and painful battles with the housing authorities to which they applied throughout the application process. Authorities of this type often demand more and more information about the violence experienced and adopt an adversarial stance highly distressing to women already traumatised by having been made homeless by violence. Women applicants may then need a high level of support and of legal representation through a long drawn out and highly contested application. Almost inevitably, protracted and upsetting housing negotiations of this kind adversely affect the children involved.

In some authorities, especially in London and in rural districts, very few women and children were accepted under the legislation and many waited for periods amounting to years, often spent in fear and uncertainty about the final outcome. Some children and women in our study were forced to move desperately from place to place in the search for housing with resulting traumatic effects on both the woman concerned and any children with her. Forced transience of this nature sometimes led to otherwise unnecessary intervention by social services and other agencies. As their periods of homelessness lengthened, women interviewees described children experiencing high levels of anxiety, fear, depression and hopelessness, and being referred to child guidance, social services, counsellors and general practitioners. These were often children who had never previously had problems of this sort.

Some women and children in the study went back home in desperation either because achieving satisfactory rehousing seemed to be so remote or because the accommodation offered was of a very poor standard. A troubling outcome was that, in the majority of these cases, either the woman or the children experienced renewed and sometimes extreme further violence.

In addition, some women who had left home due to violence but were unable to secure permanent housing faced the loss of their children to their securely housed violent partners in court proceedings, a very disturbing outcome contrary to the spirit of both the homelessness legislation (previous and current) and the emphasis on the interests of children and young people in the Children Act (Department of Health 1989).

The use of legal remedies

Increasing numbers of housing authorities have policies which demand that abused women applicants seek advice with a view to taking legal action against the violent perpetrator. This demand can be highly distressing to women who do not wish to instigate legal proceedings against their partners, or who have used them before and found them to be ineffective, and to children who may then witness their father or father-figure being taken to court. There are also financial implications with the cut-backs in the availability of legal aid.

Disturbingly, in our study, we collected some evidence that women and children seeking rehousing in various local authorities were refused any further assistance from the council once they had obtained a short-term legal order against the violent perpetrator. In some cases, their temporary accommodation was terminated as soon as the order came through, without any consultation. While this practice is not recommended by government, it may increase in the future as a rationing tool, on the grounds that the Family Law Act (Lord Chancellor's Department 1996) offers increased (though temporary and far from reliable) protection as compared with the previous domestic violence legislation.

Children and women from minority ethnic communities

The children of black women and women from minority ethnic communities forced to leave home because of violence can face particular housing difficulties. The existence of racism in the delivery of housing services has been documented (Mama 1996), although some housing authorities and associations are making efforts to improve their anti-racist practice. In general, however, the provision of interpreting and other specialised services is inadequate, and black families may face discrimination regarding the type and location of housing offers (Malos and Hague 1993). Some women and children from minority ethnic communities may need to be particularly careful about where they accept either temporary or permanent housing offers, due both to the continued incidence of racist attacks and harassment in British society and to the existence of extended family networks associated with their husbands. Such issues inevitably affect the children involved.

Positive developments

On the positive side, many local authority homelessness units and sections have now developed good policy and practice guidelines on domestic violence (see Malos and Hague 1993). These policies usually include recommendations to adopt a believing attitude to women applicants; to provide women or specialist interviewers; to conduct few or no investigations into the violence experienced; to avoid contacting perpetrators; to offer housing to women who have suffered other types of abuse apart from physical violence or who do not have children; and to secure housing of a suitable nature. Such policies, while of course implemented with varying degrees of success and commitment, are often accompanied by domestic violence training for housing workers and management. Housing associations have also implemented good practice guidelines on domestic violence with assistance from the National Federation of Housing Associations. Housing officers frequently participate in inter-agency domestic violence initiatives, which may include joint training and good practice programmes.

Key points of the Housing Act 1996

Now, of course, homelessness law has been rewritten to remove the right of homeless people to a permanent home, as documented in other chapters in this book. The ending of the duty to secure permanent accommodation for those accepted as statutorily homeless has been a severe blow for homeless people and for the organisations which help them – and for abused women and their children in particular. During the consultation process for the new 1996 Housing Act, many thousands of submissions, including strongly-argued contributions from the Women's Aid federations, were received by the Government detailing the deleterious effects of the proposals (see for example Bradburn 1994).

The Act removes separate permanent provision for homelessness beyond the new unified housing registers and limits a local authority's responsibility to a two year renewable duty to provide temporary accommodation. New regulations and guidance have mitigated some of the worst effects of the new law, for example by making it clear that homelessness is a factor which should be given due weight in the allocation of points on the waiting list for permanent accommodation. But this change is not mandatory and does not restore the situation under the previous law.

In the case of domestic violence, many local authorities have indeed introduced pointing schemes and other administrative devices to circumvent the worst-case scenario thrown up by the new Act in which abused women and children would be caught in a revolving door of homelessness and housing insecurity. However, authorities which take a more combative line towards homeless applicants are under little obligation to pursue this course of action despite the new regulations (see also Malos and Hague 1998).

The 1996 Act also limits duties applicable to so-called 'persons from abroad', and this change is anticipated to be going to have potentially dangerous consequences for immigrant and minority ethnic women and their families escaping violence here or elsewhere (WAFE 1994). The Act additionally emphasises the use of private rented accommodation by housing authorities for both temporary and permanent housing options. Shorthold and other private rented accommodation is often particularly unsuitable for women and children escaping violence due to its lack of security and of safety provisions.

On the positive side, the Act contains a comprehensive definition of domestic violence as a cause of homelessness. In addition, it offers some respite to families experiencing domestic violence who already live in local authority tenancies. Within the new grounds for repossession for nuisance and anti-social behaviour, domestic violence becomes a ground for eviction from secure tenancies and assured tenancies with social landlords (Cowan 1996; Arden and Hunter 1997).

Conclusions

Overall, however, despite a softening of the original legislation, the provisions in the 1996 Housing Act (Department of Environment 1996) which remove the statutory right to rehousing, and its insistence that it is sufficient to secure both temporary and permanent accommodation in the private rented sector, ignore the need of abused women and children for safe long term security. Neither can this safety and security be assured by action under the criminal or civil law despite recent improvements under Part IV of the Family Law Act 1996 (Lord Chancellor's Department 1996). Ultimately, for many families the only protection will be their ability to 'disappear', and for that to have any chance of success one of their key needs is for safe permanent housing.

In the coming years, we can probably expect an ever widening gap between housing authorities which will use the legislation to wash their hands of any long-term responsibility and more enlightened and conscientious authorities which will use their 'enabling' powers to ensure that women and children homeless due to violence are not disadvantaged by the new Act. However, crudely speaking, the less sympathetic authorities have been given a licence by the 1996 legislation to ignore permanent housing needs. In these areas, homelessness queues will lengthen, and refuges and other sources of temporary accommodation will probably become 'bottle-necked' and backed up. The revolving door of repeating 'blocks' of temporary accommodation beckons for women and children escaping violence in such localities.

In the meantime, funding for refuges and other women's services remains uncertain with no national funding strategy in place, despite constant lobbying by the Women's Aid federations and other bodies, although there was mention of such a strategy in the previous Labour Party policy document (Labour Party 1995) and a new government policy on violence against women is now in development.

Thus, recent UK housing policy betrays some confusion for survivors of domestic violence. This is in contradiction to the guidance issued through the Home Office, soon to be updated by the Labour government, which specifically argues that agencies need to work together to build co-ordinated strategies to secure the safety and support of abused women and their children (see Hague 1997; Hague, Malos and Dear 1996; Home Office 1995). This developing policy of multi-agency co-ordination and improved provision, despite much innovative work at local level, may be sabotaged by ambivalent housing policies. Of course, there is some hope on the horizon at the time of writing as we do not yet know what further policies the new Labour government will implement, but the evidence seems to be that, although there have been some improvements, there are no great grounds for optimism about major changes.

Meantime, though, the housing situation has worsened due to the decrease in public sector housing. Thousands of children annually continue to live in temporary accommodation solely because of violence which their mother has experienced at the hands of their father or of another man whom they may have loved and trusted. The trauma of such a life situation cannot be over-emphasised. These children continue to face an uncertain and frightening future in which a secure permanent home and safety from violence may seem like a distant mirage. No one much listens to the voices of these children. Can we, can local authorities and housing associations, and can central government afford to turn away?

Recommendations

- The restoration of the right of the statutorily homeless to permanent rehousing.

- The offering of rehousing in social rented rather than private rented housing.

- Favourable treatment under housing law for abused women who are experiencing violence from outside the home, experiencing sexual and mental violence, or do not have children.

- The ending of the use of pressure or demands for abused women to seek legal remedies before being accepted as eligible for consideration under the homelessness legislation.

- Ensuring rehousing options for women and children homeless due to violence are of good standard and in safe areas.

- The development of a national ring-fenced funding strategy for refuge provision.

- The running of refuges in conjunction with Women's Aid and other refuge providers rather than through direct management by housing associations to ensure support and advocacy as well as accommodation.

Many of these recommendations would require the reversal of the decline in publicly owned and social housing that has resulted from government housing policy since 1979.

CHAPTER 7

Homeless Adolescents

Robert Wrate and Caroline Blair

Introduction

There has been a secular shift in the demographic make-up of the homeless population in Britain. The average age is falling and the most dramatic rise in the newly homeless is in the under-25 age group (Bhugra 1996), now occupying a third of hostel places (Gill *et al.* 1996). Secular changes considered important in the genesis of homelessness in young people include the increasing fragmentation of families and family life, a possible increase in domestic violence, increased social mobility and a reduction in low income housing (Jones 1995). In Britain, the altered benefits arrangements for young people and the reduction in job opportunities for the less educated have probably also had an impact. Anecdotal experience and survey observations suggest that the life experience of young people had often been unstable before they became homeless with significant proportions reporting histories of reception into care. The somewhat glamorised stereotype of young runaways who opt positively for a homeless lifestyle has crumbled. In its place we have a growing awareness of the imperative to escape from multiple deprivation and abuse. (Feitel *et al.* 1992; Janus *et al.* 1995; Craig *et al.* 1996; Rotheram-Borus *et al.* 1996; Whitbeck, Hoyt and Ackley 1997).

As 'runaways', 'throwaways' or 'push-outs', the single young homeless have attracted sociological studies over several decades, but few studies have paid attention to mental health issues *per se*. Most earlier studies of the homeless were of adult, often middle aged, men living in hostels and lodging houses, finding high rates of psychotic illness and alcoholism (Scott 1993). However, many of the life adversities that constitute risk factors for homelessness in the young are also risk factors for mental health problems: lack of parental care, parental conflict, parental psychiatric disorder, physical and sexual abuse, and lack of social support (Garmezy and Masten 1994). For example, a British study of young people placed in children's homes found high rates of anxiety, depressive symptoms, and conduct disorders (McCann *et al.* 1996).

Three major studies of the mental health of the single young homeless people in Britain have recently been published adding significantly to knowledge about the homeless scene (Craig *et al.* 1996; Gill *et al.* 1996; Wrate and McLoughlin 1997). Our review of the health needs of the single young homeless will be presented in relation to findings from this research, with some reference to recent North American studies, and we include recommendations for service delivery and for further research.

Research methods

The three projects share a number of similar features, though each had somewhat different aims. There are many common findings, with variations in results arising more often than not from methodological differences. All were community-based projects, using survey techniques to interview homeless people in a variety of settings. All had a cross-sectional design and each employed semi-structured interviews to obtain quantitative information on a wide range of domains, including sociological data, general physical health, and mental health status. The studies differed considerably in the number of subjects interviewed, the quantity of data sought, whether qualitative information was sought or a control group was present and, finally, on whether a longitudinal design was included.

The most extensive interviews were those carried out from St Thomas' Hospital in London (UMDS), where the research study included both a control group and a longitudinal design (Craig *et al.* 1996). The antecedents and sequelae of homelessness were examined in a sample of 161 young people aged 16 to 21 attending two central London facilities in the voluntary sector, dedicated to the single young homeless (*Centrepoint* night shelter and the *London Connection*). Follow-up information about accommodation, social and health status was obtained on 86 per cent of the subjects one year later, when detailed interviews were carried out on 67 per cent of the original cohort. For comparison, an unmatched domiciled control group was obtained from two inner-city general practices. As well as establishing rates of psychiatric disorder, the study aimed to describe pathways into youth homelessness, their contacts with statutory services, associations between psychiatric disorder and social adversity, and to define factors predictive of health outcome, accommodation stability, and future employment or training.

The second study was a prevalence study carried out by the Office of Population Census Survey (OPCS), commissioned to extend the private household survey of psychiatric morbidity in Britain to cover the homeless population of all ages (Gill *et al.* 1996). Using careful sampling techniques, large numbers of homeless people were surveyed in different parts of Britain, with subjects approached at day centres for the homeless, in hostels, emergency night shelters, private leased accommodation, and at supported-accommodation units. Of necessity, a very brief structured interview was employed, with no opportunity to gather any qualitative information. The agency has published some data on a subsample of younger respondents (aged 16 to 24). Findings from this subsample (n=361) will be referred to (the full data set is archived with the Economic and Social Research Council at the University of Essex).

The third study aimed to assess the mental health needs of the population of young people either homeless or at high risk of homelessness in the city of Edinburgh (Wrate and McLoughlin 1997). Young people were recruited using an assertive outreach model of contact and networking with voluntary sector hostels, social work supported accommodation, young people's centres (i.e. children's homes), homeless outreach initiatives and the remand wing of a prison. Except for omitting the longitudinal design, the study's overall aims were rather similar to that of Craig and colleagues. As interviews were carried out in a wide variety of community settings, including on the street and in cafes (the project aimed to include low service-users), follow-up interviews were considered impracticable, and semi-structured interviews lasting no more than about an hour were employed. Quantitative data on 145 respondents aged 16 to 21 was obtained.

As noted elsewhere, the British government's statutory definition of homelessness is a narrow one, enshrining a duty to assist homeless people or those about to become homeless. All three studies used a wider dimensional definition of homelessness to include what the Royal College of Physician's working party on health and homelessness described as the 'unofficial homeless' (Connelly and Crown 1994). As well as those sleeping rough, this embraces those 'at risk', for example those in hospital or in prison with no fixed address, the 'hidden' (e.g. sleeping on friends' floors) and those staying in night shelters, hostels, and supported accommodation projects.

As Tomas and Dittmar (1995) point out, for a psychological understanding of housing in the context of homelessness, it is important to recognise that the meaning of 'home' may be very different from that of the domiciled. Participants' stories of their experiences of events are therefore also important. Both the Edinburgh and the St Thomas studies collected extensive qualitative information. Mental health problems were examined within a framework of general health and lifestyle indicators, accommodation histories; subjects' social circumstances were recorded in detail, and their existing patterns of service utilisation ascertained. In the Edinburgh study, to ensure that the meaning of the findings was understood in terms of the single young homeless' own 'social construction' (Blasi 1990), nine subjects provided 'narrative' interviews, and five focus groups of young people were convened. Last, quasi-Delphi groups (Duffield 1993; Williams and Webb 1994) with agency workers and mental health staff were used to elicit their feedback on findings and on service recommendations.

Sociodemographics and reasons for leaving home

All studies have found that young men were significantly over-represented in the young homeless population (by a factor of at least two to one). In Edinburgh, males were on average one year older, and were particularly over-represented among the long-term homeless (i.e. more than 12 months), as Craig and colleagues also found. Many adolescents do not run far from home (Abrahams and Munsall 1992). All but six per cent of the Edinburgh cohort had been born in Scotland. In the central London cohort more than half were born in the London area.

Most of the young homeless report deprived family backgrounds and in Edinburgh less than one in five of their biological parents were still living together. In Craig's study 38 per cent of the group had experienced three or more changes in care arrangements before the age of 16 (mostly precipitated by parental separations). The single young homeless are characterised by poor educational experiences, for example, half in the Edinburgh study had left school before the statutory leaving date, only a sixth had any current occupational or educational involvement. The UMDS study reported similar findings. The problem of educational deprivation is highlighted in Chapter 11.

Most respondents left home following arguments, intimidation or assault, either 'choosing' to leave or else being thrown out. In the UMDS study, 84 per cent had witnessed moderate or marked parental discord on multiple occasions, whilst severe and persistent physical abuse was reported by a third (Craig *et al.* 1996). The extent of abuse is echoed in a Canadian investigation of runaway adolescents found to be victims of chronic extreme abuse, experienced at a young age and often perpetuated by the biological mother. Female runaways were at greater risk than males for all types of abuse experience (Janus *et al.* 1995). A quarter of Craig's group described past sexual abuse, a history predictive of multiple risk behaviour in homeless youth (Rotheram-Borus *et al.* 1996). The dismal conclusion from this history of adversity is that for many homeless young people the situation they were living in whilst housed was the problem – homelessness may well be a solution (Tomas and Dittmar 1995).

Past residential care experience

In the British studies, up to half the single young homeless had social work 'in care' experience. The strength of this association has been the focus of two earlier studies of Canadian youth (Raychaba 1989) and in Manchester (Wiggans 1989). The care system appears to foster an over-reliance on others, where survival skills are acquired for group rather than independent living. Residents are frequently ill prepared for independent living with limited problem solving skills (Boulton 1993), poor access to education (Power *et al.* 1995) and the local authority support for care-leavers is often inadequate (Social Services Inspectorate 1997). There are often precipitous departures from unstable or chaotic residential units with disconnection of attachments. In the UMDS study, the ability to plan ahead was an important predictor of stable housing at the one year follow-up.

In spite of the extended requirements described in recent Children's Act legislation, with the immense pressures on the care system there seems little likelihood of young people having much scope to correct mistakes by obtaining further social work support or re-entering residential care. Even allowing for increased investment for the over-16s, a major re-think of residential care aims for adolescents is required. This is likely to have considerable implications for staff training.

Instability of accommodation after leaving home

A striking feature of the young homeless scene is the instability of accommodation after the first breakdown. In the Edinburgh study half the group had been in their present accommodation for eight weeks or less, and 25 per cent reported having had more than ten accommodation addresses since the age of ten. Craig and colleagues found that a history of childhood adversity and duration of homelessness beyond two years was significantly associated with mental health problems.

Poor quality accommodation is a recurrent theme with unsupported district council tenancies singled out for particular opprobrium. Unstable peer relationships often seemed to play a major role in the breakdown of shared accommodation. In the UMDS study length of homelessness predicted stable housing at the one year follow-up, irrespective of whether or not respondents had experienced periods of stable housing in between.

One of the characteristics of the older homeless population is that contact with family members has been lost. In young people the picture is more variable. In Edinburgh, a fifth of the sample had no contact with their mother in the previous week but half had been in touch. Young women reported more contacts (and were more likely to keep in contact with previous carers, particularly foster parents), but in general family communication was often experienced as difficult. The earlier young people had been received into care the more likely they were to report difficulties in communicating with family members.

The achievement of housing stability is an important goal, and even when living out with their own families local connections seem to play a useful stabilising role. For example, some respondents in Edinburgh referred to family members helping them to find housing provision, whilst those in the UMDS follow-up who had achieved stable housing were more likely to have been from the London area. Females, black, and minority ethnic respondents fared better overall, perhaps because of their closer family ties.

Improved community resources for families would help improve the situation, whilst more direct support for young people living independently (including crisis counselling, and helping them plan ahead) may reduce the rate of breakdown of tenancies. Without improved housing stability, no accommodation can feel like 'home'.

Physical health problems

Writing from a psychiatric perspective on the service needs of the mentally ill homeless, Bachrach (1992) stated that 'the need for medical and surgical care in this population is so staggering that it falls well outside the bounds of what a traditional mental health service might offer' (p.459). Her observations, directed at the adult population, apply as forcefully to the young homeless. The Edinburgh and London studies reported high rates of self reported illness: stomach problems, headaches, aching joints, loss of appetite, persistent tonsillitis, chronic bronchitis, back pain, skin trouble and epilepsy (Wrate 1997). In Edinburgh, perceived physical health status was well below age-matched norms and 40 per cent of the cohort complained of moderate to severe pain in the previous month. Strikingly high rates of sleep disturbance and tiredness were found in both the Edinburgh and OPCS survey. Low energy and tiredness were associated with particular lifestyle factors: the frequent experience of hunger, irregular eating habits and irregular or disturbed sleep patterns.

As the physical health of the general population has improved, Rutter and Smith (1990) describe a widening gap between mental health and physical health in post-war generations of children. There is no evidence of this trend in the young homeless. Instead it seems likely that health inequalities persisting from childhood are present (Benzeval, Judge and Whitehead 1995), general health impairment compounded further by poor housing and diets, and by risk taking behaviour (Rotheram-Borus et al. 1996; Kral et al. 1997).

To be effective, health care must adopt a 'holistic' approach. Without initiatives to ensure continuity of primary care services, the typical homeless individual's combination of stoicism and transient accommodation will constitute a formidable obstacle to improved general health. Improved services for the single young homeless are only likely to develop by joint commissioning (health, social services, housing, and voluntary agencies), which should proceed with the expectation that statutory agencies will work collaboratively with voluntary sector providers (Timms and Balazs 1997).

Mental health problems

What is mental health? Goodman (1997) has stirred up debate on the medicalisation of certain health problems, which although included in the main psychiatric classification systems, could be considered primarily as social problems: conduct disorders, anti-social disorder, and substance abuse. Since these are commonly associated with childhood adversity, their inclusion in mental health surveys of the young homeless inevitably increase prevalence rates. Survey findings therefore need to be interpreted with care. The UMDS study finding that two-thirds were suffering from a psychiatric disorder, was strongly affected by the research team's decision to include both drug taking and behavioural problems as indicators of psychiatric disorder. More than half their cohort (55%) were given a retrospective diagnosis of conduct disorder (almost four times the rate for their control group), half of which were considered severe and persistent.

However, drug taking, even substance dependency, was not uncommon in their control group and at follow-up some non-users were taking drugs whilst some previous users had stopped. The OPCS survey and the Edinburgh study adopted a different perspective on drug taking and anti-social behaviour, each study electing to consider both behaviours as lifestyle indicators. This is reflected in our review of research findings for mental health problems, which considers findings for psychosis and for emotional, 'neurotic', or mood disorders separately from substance use/ abuse disorders.

Craig and colleagues reported a three per cent prevalence of schizophrenia, and in Edinburgh there was one young person with probable psychosis and a couple of distinctly odd young people of uncertain diagnosis. Although higher than estimates for the total population, (0.5%) these rates are far lower than recent estimates (9%–30%) of the prevalence of schizophrenia in adult residents in homeless hostels in the UK (Marshall 1996).

Using a structured psychiatric interview, ten per cent of the Edinburgh respondents were found to be suffering from a major depressive episode, none of whom were receiving any treatment in spite of fairly high attendance at their general practitioners (Blair and Wrate 1997). Using a broader definition of illness, the UMDS study reported a depression rate three times as high, and found that at one year follow up those who had recovered from depression were replaced by a similar number with new onsets. A third of the Edinburgh sample reported a past episode of depression, the presence of poor physical health perhaps increasing the likelihood of depressive illness being overlooked, for example where presentations are complex.

To adapt to the differing interviewing conditions in the OPCS survey, different methods of screening for psychiatric disorder were employed. Even the most in-depth of their measures (the Revised Clinical Interview Schedule, Lewis et al. 1992), which identifies up to six types of 'neurotic disorder', was briefer than those used in the Edinburgh and UMDS research. Nevertheless, a rate of 36 per cent is reported. These British studies broadly confirm earlier North American studies that had also used structured psychiatric interviews, which have reported rates of major depressive disorder of up to 49 per cent in this age group (see for example Schaffer and Caton 1984; Feitel et al. 1992), In summary, the rates of depression in the single young homeless have invariably been twice or more than the rate expected in the community (Cooper and Goodyer 1993; Kessler *et al.* 1994; West and Sweeting 1996).

Both the OPCS survey and the Edinburgh study produced the same two similar unexpected findings. First, no association was found between reported social contacts and depression. Community studies of domiciled individuals invariably demonstrate an inverse relationship between social support and depression (see for example Kovacs 1996). This appears not to apply to the young homeless. It is likely that a combination of factors is responsible. For example, social adversity may be so great and social support so poor within the homeless that additive effects for mental illness may be minimal. In addition, some vulnerable homeless individuals may function better with less social contact. Second, similar rates of mental health problems for young men and women were found. Community surveys consistently show a two to one female excess after early adolescence (Angold and Worthman 1993). This finding, which needs replicating, may be due to sampling characteristics of the two studies.

Parasuicidal acts among the single young homeless attract much staff concern and, we learnt, highly critical attitudes from peers. Community surveys have shown that suicidal thoughts, if not acts, are relatively common in the young, estimates varying according to exactly what question is asked. However, the lifetime prevalence of recurring suicidal thoughts in the Edinburgh cohort was 54 per cent (Blair and Wrate 1997), a rate at least twice that found in a community survey of young people in Glasgow (West and Sweeting 1996). Furthermore, 28 per cent of the Edinburgh cohort had made an attempt on their life, a rate seven times that found in the Glasgow community survey. The UMDS homeless cohort in London demonstrated a four fold increase over the domiciled control group; other surveys of the young homeless showing rates of suicidal acts between 28 per cent and 46 per cent (Schaffer and Caton, 1984; Mundy *et al.* 1990; Feitel *et al.* 1992).

In summary, there is now well replicated data indicating high levels of psychological disorder in homeless young people, however 'disorder' is defined and whatever methodology is used. The single young homeless are very vulnerable to mental health problems, and many demonstrate limited coping strategies. Effective interventions are likely to be community-based, providing outreach services and, whenever it is possible to do so, offering problem solving treatment approaches over psycho-pharmacological treatments. Such initiatives are also likely to improve the widely-held negative image of formal mental health services. Improved access to specialist mental health services is only likely to be achieved by the establishment of outreach or detached health workers, offering direct access with outreach clinics at the main hostels and regular staff liaison. Young people frequently take several months of turbulence and activity before stabilising on to a more settled course, which makes a service based on a model of high short-term involvement followed by quick closure untenable.

Last, more thought is required to ensure an appropriate level involvement of mental health services for young people presenting with behaviour and impulse-control problems. Some of these problems may be secondary to benzodiazepine withdrawal, result from irritability associated with unrecognised mood disorders, or reflect an untreated attention-deficit disorder.

Drug use and other lifestyle indicators

Relatively low levels of alcohol dependency were found in the Edinburgh and UMDS cohorts compared to what has been found in older cohorts of homeless people (Scott 1993). On the other hand, the widespread use of illicit drugs in the younger homeless is a universal finding (Craig *et al.* 1966; Gill *et al.* 1996; Greene, Ennett and Ringwalt 1997; Wrate *et al.* 1997). In the OPCS study, the use of drugs was greatest among the 16 to 24 years old cohort. An American study found that a cohort of street youth had higher rates of substance use than adolescents in night shelters or those with previous homeless histories, and these in turn had higher rates than young people who had never been homeless (Greene *et al.* 1997).

Comorbidity between substance *dependence* and mental health problems was evident in all the three British studies but this did not apply to substance *use*. For example, in the Edinburgh cohort a strong association was found between substance use (e.g. units of alcohol intake, cigarette consumption, amount of marijuana in the last month), and number of changes of address since 15 years old, but not with measures of ill-health. By contrast, for those with a very high overall drug intake a clear relationship with current depression was found. Similarly, 45 per cent of the UMDS cohort with a neurotic or psychotic mental illness were regularly abusing one or more substances of addiction, little different from the OPCS study. The close association between depression and substance dependence has also been found in many community surveys of young people (Kovacs 1996) but the meaning of the association remains unclear (Windle and Windle 1997).

Even with a longitudinal design, Craig and colleagues have not yet been able to establish the meaning of the significant relationship they found between substance abuse disorders and failure to achieve stable housing. Rather than arising from a direct link between the two, the relationship may have arisen from a third factor, for example their initiative being impaired by comorbid depression, or perhaps impulsivity contributing to both housing instability and drug taking. The two main explanations usually offered for the association between depression and drug abuse are either that such dependence reflects inappropriate coping strategies, depressed subjects using substances to self-medicate (Gruber, Pope and Brown 1996), or that the main effect arises from high levels of substance abuse acting to precipitate or exacerbate mental illness in vulnerable young people. The 'narrative' interviews in Edinburgh suggested both occur, but cross-sectional studies cannot demonstrate causal links, least of all their direction.

Last, a number of research groups have expressed concern about the high prevalence of sexual risk behaviour found in young homeless cohorts. For example, early sexual intercourse, unprotected sex, exchange of sex for material gain, and a majority reporting sexual experience under the influence of drink or drugs (Craig et al. 1996; Rotherham-Borus et al. 1996; Kral et al. 1997; Wrate et al. 1997). All these are associated with a high risk of HIV infection. In the Edinburgh cohort, three-quarters of respondents reported unsafe sexual experience, and those most likely to be at risk (because of frequent sexual partners) indicated least interest in contraceptive advice. The meaning of this association is unclear. Is there a direct link between homelessness and high risk sexual behaviour or are both precipitated by a third factor such as impulsivity, depression or poor problem solving?

Fresh approaches are required to promote the health and well-being of the single young homeless, especially in relation to conflict and risk taking behaviour. For example, a pilot action-research project on 'peer-educators' could be set up, perhaps focusing on drug use, safe and non-abusive sexual practice, and the management of conflict within relationships (Fors and Jarvis 1995). Again, it must be emphasised that service models based on intensive short-term input are unlikely to succeed.

Conclusion

Well-conducted research over the last ten years has conclusively demonstrated a close association between social disadvantage and health impairment, including among the young single homeless, where high levels

---

Box 7.1 Two case studies

A 20-year-old young man on benefits, whose self-report measures indicated poor subjective health, poor appetite and weight loss, feeling constantly worn out and with little exercise tolerance. He was obviously frail at interview and in apparent pain; he reported many previous illness episodes, with poorly healed previous injuries and was expecting that his health was more likely to decline further than improve. He had left home at 14, unable to get on with his step-father whom he held responsible for his mother's poor health, and stayed with various relatives before becoming homeless. He had experienced many forms of homelessness, including rough sleeping, hostels, friends' floors, and a failed council tenancy before his current supported-accommodation flat. He was a considerable user of methadone, marijuana, and temazepam. Though he reported himself as sociable he felt unable to confide in others; his daily life was characterised by sleep disturbance and inactivity. He was found to be suffering from a major depressive disorder, with several previous episodes, some of which were associated with overdoses, and he was clearly still deeply affected by the death of a close friend. His self-esteem seemed very low and he spoke of being ashamed of the condition the interviewer had found him in.

A 19-year-old young woman who had lived at fourteen different addresses, hostels and so on since leaving home at 15 following sexual abuse. She also described poor general health and previous rough sleeping, and reported experience of being raped and having worked as a prostitute. She had first taken an overdose when eleven years old, with several episodes of depression and overdoses since, and a history of major substance dependency. She reported disturbing thoughts with a sexual theme, a paranoid sensitivity, and was worried that something was wrong with her mind. Bulimic episodes and self-cutting had been present for several years, and she was found to be currently suffering from a major depressive episode.

---

of both mental health problems and physical health disorders have been found. Since earlier family adversity is a very common finding among the homeless, it is not clear how far the high levels of morbidity represent the extension into young adulthood of disorders established in childhood. Nevertheless, it seems unlikely that their contemporary social circumstances are not contributing to their impaired well-being. Depressive illness, perhaps comorbid with other mental health problems, appears to be the most common psychiatric disorder. Although depression is eminently treatable, only a minority of affected adolescents appear to have received any treatment. Comorbid physical complaints may mask depression, although community studies have demonstrated that depression is often unrecognised even in community samples of domiciled adolescents. However, there is widespread agreement that the homeless experience many barriers to services, and equity of access seems only possible where services go out to them on their own territory. Without outreach services, no adolescent mental health service is likely to improve the situation described above. At the time of writing, no single service in the UK offers this.

Recommendations

Two measures are required to reduce the risk of future homelessness among care-leavers:

- First, it is essential to enhance their individual problem-solving skills during their period in care, especially their capacity to plan ahead and to manage conflict.
- Second, as the SSI report has emphasised, initiatives are required that greatly improve their after-care support.

Such initiatives are likely to contribute to future accommodation stability, but additional measures to assist housing stability for all vulnerable young people are required. These include improving the quality of the housing provided and, where appropriate, actively supporting single young homeless people's family contacts.

Improved health care is only likely to be achieved by proactive interventions, adopting a holistic approach and provided on an outreach basis. Such provision would assist the de-stigmatisation of mental health services, and improve the recognition of mental health problems, particularly depression.

Service models based on short-term inputs are unlikely to be cost-effective. Innovative schemes are required, especially in relation to the identification of treatable mental health problems in presentations of drug misuse and impulse control problems. The use of 'peer-educators' should be considered. Joint commissioning of services is also recommended.

Acknowledgments

The Edinburgh study of the single young homeless was funded by the Primary Care Development Fund of the Department of Health at the Scottish Office. It was carried out by a research team at the Young People's Unit, Royal Edinburgh Hospital, in association with the Homeless Team at Lothian Health's Primary Care Services.

CHAPTER 8

Effects of Changes in Housing Legislation

Pat Niner

This chapter looks at aspects of housing policy and law as they affect homeless families in England and Wales. It looks first at homelessness legislation, including recent changes, and explores how this essentially 'defines' homelessness. It then describes some of the practical outcomes of the implementation of homelessness policy for homeless families, and finally identifies some important issues for the future.

Homelessness legislation in England and Wales

Before 1977, homelessness was not strictly a 'housing' matter – welfare authorities had a duty to provide temporary accommodation 'for persons who are in urgent need thereof, being need arising in circumstances which could not reasonably have been foreseen or in such other circumstances as the authority may in a particular case determine' (National Assistance Act 1948, section 21(1)). There was no complementary duty to provide any form of permanent housing for homeless people, and council housing (the main source of rented housing for poorer and needy people) was under the control of separate housing authorities. Despite central government urges towards greater sharing of responsibilities between local social services (formerly welfare) and housing authorities, the picture was generally very variable over the country, and basically highly unsatisfactory with families being separated in temporary accommodation and children at risk of being taken into care simply because their parents lacked accommodation.

The introduction of the Housing (Homeless Persons) Act 1977 – later consolidated into Part III of the Housing Act 1985 – changed all this. Very broadly, Part III placed on local housing authorities a duty to secure accommodation for persons who were homeless and who had not become homeless intentionally and who were in priority need. Establishing homelessness, priority need and intentionality required the authority to make enquiries, and the outcome of these enquiries determined the extent of the duty owed to the applicant. Enquiries could also be made into an applicant's 'local connection' which could affect which authority took responsibility for rehousing. While enquiries were being made, authorities had to provide temporary accommodation for applicants whom it had reason to believe were actually homeless and in priority need.

The full rehousing duty to an unintentionally homeless applicant in priority need was 'to secure that accommodation becomes available for his occupation' (Housing Act 1985 section 65(2)). Although not spelled out in the law, this was normally secured through the allocation of a council tenancy or (latterly) a nomination to a housing association tenancy. To facilitate such allocation of council housing, section 22 of the 1985 Act included persons to whom a duty was owed under section 65 (homelessness) as one of the categories of applicants to be given reasonable preference by authorities in the selection of tenants. Thus a specific link was established between homelessness and rehousing provisions.

Definitions of 'homelessness', 'priority need', 'intentional homelessness' and 'local connection' were based on the Act itself, advice given by the Secretary of State in the form of Codes of Guidance (three editions were issued between 1977 and 1991) and developing case law. Together they essentially created a legal construct of the 'homeless' who could expect help, including rehousing. However, the legal framework of definitions left significant scope for local discretion which could mean that applicants in identical circumstances were treated differently in different areas.

Two definitions are particularly important here in limiting the potential scope of assistance to homeless people – of the priority needs groups and 'intentional homelessness'. Priority need was determined by presence in the applicant household of dependent children or a pregnant woman, or someone 'vulnerable' by reason of old age, mental illness or handicap or physical disability, or other special reason. Households made homeless by an emergency (fire or flood) were also in priority need. Not surprisingly most accepted homeless households were families with children or included a pregnant woman.

Deciding whether homelessness was 'intentional' proved to be the most controversial area in the legislation, and a large body of complex case law developed as local authority decisions were challenged. The issue was of more than academic interest since it directly affected the duty placed on the local authority and thus the rehousing chances of an applicant. The duty owed to an intentionally homeless applicant was to provide advice, assistance and temporary accommodation – not to secure permanent accommodation. In order to be intentionally homeless, the applicant had to have deliberately done something (or failed to do something) as a consequence of which accommodation was lost which it would otherwise have been reasonable for the applicant to continue to occupy. At its crudest, homelessness resulting from eviction due to rent arrears arising from a deliberate refusal to pay rent which the applicant could afford, despite warning that this could mean that the home would be lost, could be seen as intentional.

Homelessness because of eviction for arrears arising from genuine financial difficulties (perhaps following a relationship breakdown or illness) should not be considered as intentional. While the question of intention arose in a minority of cases, issues were rarely as straightforward as the example suggests. The existence of the intention provision may have deterred some applicants, making it more important than official figures suggest.

Reviews of homelessness legislation

Homelessness legislation was reviewed by the Conservative Government in the late 1980s (Department of Environment 1989). Despite widely held expectations that changes would be proposed to make the law more restrictive, the Review concluded that the 'legislation has worked reasonably well and should remain in place as a "long-stop" to help those who through no fault of their own have become homeless'(Department of Environment 1989, p.21). No legislative change was proposed, although an amended Code of Guidance was recommended to help secure greater consistency between authorities in the discharge of their duties. This Code was issued in 1991 and included much more attention to the quality of the homelessness service offered and customer care aspects as well as providing more detailed and explicit guidance on interpreting the legislation.

However, demands for review had not been silenced. A consultation paper was published in January 1994 which set out the Government's proposals 'for ensuring fairer access to local authority and housing association tenancies' (Department of Environment 1994: para 1.1). The main line of argument was that the scale of rehousing through homelessness had been much greater than was envisaged when legislation was introduced in 1977. Priority in allocations given to homeless people had confused the safety net aspect of the legislation with a fast-track to a council tenancy, thereby distorting allocations. This was perceived as a problem because homelessness, while undoubtedly evidence of a short-term crisis requiring a safety net, may not necessarily represent evidence of a long-term need for social rented housing.

The consultation paper also referred to other issues of fairness including meeting the needs of 'couples seeking to establish a good home in which to start and raise a family' (such a couple would be unlikely to get help through homelessness legislation because they would not fall into a priority need group) and not penalising someone who 'takes the initiative in finding alternative accommodation' rather than applying to the authority as homeless (Department of Environment 1994, p.4). The overall intention of the reforms proposed was to put 'all those with long-term housing needs on the same footing, while providing a safety net for emergency and pressing needs' (Department of Environment 1995, p.37).

The reasoning in these consultation papers is riddled with value judgements and largely unsupported contentions – for example, for how many homeless people is homelessness a short-term crisis? do local authorities give unthinking priority to homeless applicants? do homeless people never look for alternative accommodation for themselves before turning to the local authority? However, the proposals in the papers were largely carried through and enacted in Parts VI and VII of the Housing Act 1996 (Arden and Hunter 1996).

The Housing Act 1996 and homelessness

Given the slant of the consultation papers described above, it is not surprising that the 1996 Act tried to separate the safety net aspect of homelessness provisions from the more general issues of allocation of long-term social tenancies. Part VII deals with the former and Part VI with the latter, though it is essential to look at both parts together as they interact. There were three main changes of relevance. The nature of the full homelessness rehousing duty was changed; all new council tenancies and housing association nominations had to be made from a statutory housing register; and homelessness *per se* ceased to be a category to be accorded 'reasonable preference' in the allocation of tenancies. Definitions of homelessness, priority need and intention remained broadly unchanged, as did the duty to provide 'interim accommodation' pending enquiries.

Under Section 193 of the 1996 Act an authority has the duty 'to secure that accommodation is available for occupation by the applicant', where the applicant is in priority need and has become homeless unintentionally. This duty lasts for a 'minimum period' of two years, with discretion to continue provision beyond this if, following review, the applicant still meets the relevant criteria. Accommodation provided under Section 193 is intended as a safety net; during the minimum period of its provision the assumption is that the applicant can find long-term accommodation in the private or social sectors.

Section 197 provides that the two year duty does not apply where the local authority is satisfied that suitable alternative accommodation exists for the applicant in their area. The duty under Section 197 is to provide such advice and assistance as is reasonably required to enable the applicant to secure accommodation for him or herself. An amendment following the election of a Labour Government in May 1997 meant that any accommodation would have to be available for at least two years to be 'suitable'. This implies that, if private tenancies are to be used, the authority will require some sort of assurance from the landlord of continuing availability (Campbell 1997). This change has introduced greater specificity into what was previously a very vague area.

Part VI of the Housing Act 1996 requires local authorities to keep a Register of qualifying applicants from which allocations of social housing must be made. It gives the secretary of state powers to prescribe categories of people who must be included on the Register and who are disqualified from it. Regulations made under the Act mean that certain people owed duties under Part VII (homelessness) must appear of the Register, while the 'statutory' disqualifications relate to categories of persons subject to immigration control. Local authorities can, in addition, set their own eligibility criteria so long as the statutory provisions are met. They could therefore apply local residence conditions, exclude those not in housing need or guilty of some anti-social behaviour.

Local authorities must adopt a local allocation system. Within this certain groups must be given reasonable preference, although their relative priority is a matter for local discretion. The reasonable preference groups were set out in section 167 of the Housing Act 1996 and did not include homeless people owed a duty under Part VII. However, the listed categories were broadly drawn and could encompass most circumstances which might lead to home loss, or which might be experienced while in temporary accommodation provided for the minimum period under Part VII.

The incoming Labour Government re-introduced certain groups owed a duty under Part VII (homelessness) as a reasonable preference category within an authority's allocation scheme. How the needs of the homeless and others are to be weighed is a matter for the local allocation scheme. Thus the Housing Act 1996, while not fundamentally affecting who is defined as homeless and in priority need, has changed the legal rights of homeless families. It remains to be seen how far any change in outcomes will result.

Outcomes for homeless families

Regular statistical returns, and a number of research studies over the years have traced the outcomes of the homelessness legislation. Homeless acceptances (broadly applicants found to be unintentionally homeless and in priority need) grew steadily to the peak quarter ending March 1992 when 38,150 households were accepted in England. After that date the trend was slowly downward. The decline was perhaps attributable to growing opportunities in the private rented and housing association sectors. Some thought it reflected the growing unpopularity of council housing in certain areas which deterred people with any choice from applying (Mullins and Niner 1996).

Two-thirds of accepted households during the mid 1990s were families including dependent children or a pregnant woman. This is a direct consequence of the way in which the priority need categories are defined. Because of this, the assessment process is somewhat simpler for families with children suffering home loss who do not have to prove that they are 'vulnerable' as childless households do.

However, it is apparent that many children in families are likely to have gone through a period of acute stress and disruption of family life before they were accepted as homeless. Statistics available on reasons for homelessness show that the single most significant reason was because parents, relatives or friends were no longer willing or able to accommodate the applicant. This reason accounted for over four out of every ten acceptances in 1990, but had declined to about three out of ten by 1996. Homelessness attributable to violent or non-violent relationship breakdown increased over the same period from about one in six to one in four acceptances. Other reasons for homelessness (for example, home loss because of mortgage or other arrears

and loss of private tenancies) have generally been less significant and have varied over time with housing market trends.

The use of temporary accommodation, and especially shared accommodation in hostels, refuges or bed and breakfast hotels, has been one of the most criticised aspects of homelessness procedures, particularly as it affects children and their families. Some local authorities used temporary accommodation much more extensively than others. For example, Niner (1989) found that Birmingham had accepted 2602 households as homeless in the first six months of 1987, but had only 85 households in temporary accommodation, none in bed and breakfast.

By contrast, the London Borough of Hillingdon accepted 201 households over the same six months, but had 270 households in temporary accommodation of whom just over half were in bed and breakfast hotels (Niner 1989). Similar variations have been observed in the length of time a family might expect to spend in temporary accommodation before being rehoused. A survey of English and Welsh local authorities at the end of 1993 produced individual estimates of the average time applicants could expect to spend in temporary accommodation which varied from less than a week to three years, with the longest average stays in some London Boroughs and authorities in the south of England (Mullins and Niner 1996). Where an applicant needed unusually large or specialised housing, a longer wait could be involved almost anywhere because few suitable vacancies arise.

Some of these differences observed between authorities in the use of temporary accommodation could be traced to the different relative priority given to homeless households in the allocation of permanent accommodation, but more fundamentally they stemmed from the very different supply and demand pressures in different areas.

In terms of change over time, the use of temporary accommodation peaked in September 1992 when 65,500 households were accommodated in England. Numbers fell by a third to the end of December 1994 with a subsequent slight fall. The type of accommodation used for temporary housing also changed significantly over time, with a general trend towards better quality and self-contained accommodation, often involving some sort of leasing arrangement making use of private sector property. In particular, the use of bed and breakfast hotels declined both absolutely and proportionately during the 1990s. For example, peak use of bed and breakfast was recorded at the end of September 1991 (13,550 households) and had declined to 3940 by the end of March 1997. In early 1997, about one household in ten in temporary accommodation was in bed and breakfast compared with almost half in June 1987 (West 1997). Temporary accommodation was not always provided within the local authority area; out-of-borough placement was especially common in London. The type and location of temporary accommodation allocated obviously affected family experiences and the extent of disruption involved.

Homelessness provided an important channel of access to local authority tenancies. In the peak year 1992/93 over one in three new council tenants (35%) were housed as homeless. By 1995/96 this proportion had fallen to 28 per cent, but still exceeded half in London (Wilcox 1997). Looking only at family sized accommodation shows still higher proportions of council house vacancies being allocated to homeless households. Homeless families also made up a significant proportion of the nominations to housing association tenancies made by local authorities. However, research found that, while homelessness often gave priority for speedy rehousing, applicants' choice was normally restricted (single offer policies) and the system could work so that homeless people ended up in the least desirable properties and estates (Mullins and Niner 1996).

In summary, the homelessness legislation benefited families with children in the most extreme need of housing (so long as they had not made themselves homeless 'intentionally') by providing a priority route to a social tenancy. The process, however, was not necessarily without pain. The bureaucratic procedures involved in applying could be seen as degrading (Thomas and Niner 1989); temporary accommodation could be poor in quality, overcrowded and unsuited to family life, and disruptive of local links and networks; and the end product could be relatively unattractive. By the mid 1990s the homelessness service and the quality of temporary accommodation had improved (Mullins and Niner 1996), but there seems to have been little similar improvement in the quality of permanent accommodation available at the end of the process.

And with the Housing Act 1996?

As noted above, the Housing Act 1996 changed the legal rights of homeless people. It is still too early though to trace implications into outcomes for families and children. Research was carried out on behalf of the Department of the Environment, Transport and the Regions to provide a baseline of local authority allocation policies and practices before the introduction of the new legislation (Griffiths *et al.* 1997). As yet, no comparable 'post-Act' study has been undertaken. A small case study based project was commissioned by Shelter on the early impacts of the new Act which provided some indications, but preceded the most recent regulation changes introduced by the new Government (Niner 1997).

In some ways, things seem to have remained broadly the same as before. Early homelessness returns show, for example, that little has changed in relation to priority need or reasons for homelessness, or the types of temporary accommodation being used by local authorities. The Shelter early impact research found that contrasting case study authorities had tried, in devising their new allocation schemes, to replicate the sort of balance between the needs of homeless households and other applicants achieved under the old legislation (Niner 1997).

However, there does seem to have been a fall in the overall number of homeless applications and acceptances since the 1996 Act which is larger than might have been anticipated from trends alone. For example, there was a fall of nine per cent in the number of acceptances in priority need in England between the second quarter 1996 and the second quarter 1997. This is a sharp drop which contrasts with relative stability in recent years (London Research Centre 1998). The fall in applications and acceptances might reflect lower customer demand in the face of growing unpopularity of social rented housing or wider options in the private sector. It might, however, also be due to the new legislation.

The Shelter early impact research revealed that some of the case study authorities had aimed to reduce the number of applicants dealt with through homelessness channels by improving their access to rehousing through the Register. One case study authority was seeking, in its information leaflets, to get over the message that homelessness was no longer a direct route to a council house. Clearly, such approaches might have the effect of reducing the number of applications as homeless.

While it is probably comforting for politicians and housing professionals to see homelessness figures falling, it is not entirely clear whether such a development should be seen as good or bad for the families concerned. On the plus side, an allocation through the Register could avoid the upset and trauma of a homelessness application and investigations; it could give the applicant wider choice of property or location, perhaps at the expense of a longer wait.

However, some commentators take the view that deterring applications runs the risk of concealing genuine housing needs and homelessness. Some argue that applicants 'will not receive the detailed assessment given during a homelessness assessment' and that particular housing needs and vulnerabilities may not be picked up (Bacon 1998, p.36). Certainly homelessness assessments tend to be more exhaustive than those for the Register, but it remains debateable whether any needs revealed would be met more quickly or fully with homelessness status.

In parts of the country with large numbers of asylum seekers and others from abroad and subject to immigration control, the statutory exclusions from housing assistance are clearly highly significant both for families and local authorities. Temporary accommodation secured under Children or National Assistance Act powers may be of lower quality than that used by housing authorities dealing with homeless people. Stress and uncertainty are extreme, and longer-term housing prospects depend on immigration decisions. While families are affected in this way, the Shelter research suggested that the majority were single people. Four-fifths of the asylum seekers caseload in one Borough were single people (Niner 1997).

One clear effect of the new legislation has been to increase variability of policy and practice between local authorities. After a period of apparently increasing consistency in homelessness practices, the new Act seems to have significantly reversed this trend in a number of ways. One of the most important areas of differing practice is whether and how Section 197 (the suitable alternative accommodation clause) is used. The Shelter research revealed very different practices in this area. The subsequent changes in definition of suitable accommodation under Section 197 (see above) may have reduced the scope for this kind of difference of approach, but will not have removed it. It seems likely, therefore, that the implications of legislative change for homeless families could be significantly affected by where they live and the particular combination of policy and practice adopted by their local authority.

Some issues for the future

The Government is still committed to reviewing homelessness legislation, possibly with a view to restoring some of the rights taken away by the Housing Act 1996. However, at the time of writing (summer 1998) no concrete proposals have been made, nor has parliamentary time been made available. So, what changes would most benefit homeless families with children?

In some ways, current legislation is relatively favourable to families with children. Families with children fall clearly within the British socio-legal construct of 'homelessness' (unless they are deemed to have become homeless intentionally), and are therefore eligible for all available assistance. While campaigners for homeless single and childless people must still argue about eligibility, definitions of vulnerability and so on, this is not really a battle for families. For families it might be argued that more now depends on the process of applying as homeless, and what can be expected at the end of that process.

The homelessness process

As noted above, the process of losing a home is likely to be highly stressful for those involved, especially where friction and violence are involved. Even an apparently less painful home loss because of arrears is often the culmination of months or years of struggle and worry, sometimes compounded by relationship breakdown, unemployment or ill health. Children experiencing such a series of events will be inherently vulnerable. In these circumstances, it is especially important that the administrative and other processes surrounding a homelessness application do not add to the strains on family life.

Some of the things to be considered include:

- Providing speedy and accessible housing advice and assistance so that home loss can be prevented if possible. The Housing Act 1996 placed a duty of local authorities to provide a homelessness advisory service; as yet there has been no research about the quality and effectiveness of services being offered, though this is clearly important.

- Improving the quality of service to homeless applicants. The range here is enormous, from quite small things like providing somewhere for children to play, through ensuring good access to offices and short waiting periods for interviews, to making assessments as efficient, unintrusive and sympathetic as possible.

- Reducing the uncertainty of the process for the applicant. This would include provision of explanatory material and information, and keeping applicants up to date with the progress of their application. It is particularly important to tell people what sort of accommodation they can expect, and how long it will take.

- Providing better quality, self-contained temporary accommodation for homeless families. Considerable progress has been made in this area, though more needs doing in terms of sympathetic allocations to retain links with family, schools and other services wherever possible. These points are, of course, particularly important where families can expect to be in temporary accommodation for some time.

- Ensuring that family support is available where needed on health, education and social matters. While authorities and departments are apparently getting better at sharing information and working together, significant difficulties can still arise because of scarce resources and differing service priorities.

These are areas where legislation *per se* is not the whole answer. Since 1991, homelessness Codes of Guidance have put increasing stress on service quality and co-operation between agencies. These points were re-stated and strengthened in the Code issued to accompany the 1996 Act (Department of Environment – Department of Health 1996). Research has suggested that service quality has improved (Mullins and Niner 1996) during the 1990s. It is important that momentum is kept up, whatever changes in law may or may not take place.

Making a 'home'

Perhaps the most important challenge for the future is to put the 'home' into the homelessness service for families. For many years the main concern has been to ensure that a homeless family gets accommodation – or a roof over their heads. Several factors are now combining to shift emphasis from this relatively simple objective towards the more complex one of providing a home in which successful family life can be sustained.

Even though the Housing Act 1996 has reduced the rights of homeless people in securing permanent housing, it seems probable that most will still ultimately be housed in rented local authority or housing association accommodation, allocated through the Housing Register. The Shelter research on early impacts suggested that, in some areas, restrictions on choice of type of property or location and single offer policies for homeless people were still a feature of the revised allocation systems (Niner 1997). In turn, this suggests that homeless people, including families, may find themselves being offered the less attractive and popular properties and estates.

At the same time, there is growing concern over falling demand for social rented accommodation. Local authorities and housing associations over wide areas of England experience difficulties in letting their least attractive houses and flats. Sometimes this may be due to poor physical conditions, sometimes to social conditions on estates and fear of vandalism, crime and neighbour nuisance. Social segregation on council estates is growing, apparent in high levels of unemployment, poverty and benefit dependency, and in concentrations of lone parent families. Children's educational attainments and attendance records are significantly below average on such estates (Power and Tunstall 1995). Difficult-to-let housing can co-exist with high levels of homelessness and apparent housing need; the fear is that homeless and other desperate families will be housed in the least attractive areas because the offer will come quickly and they have no choice but to accept it.

In these circumstances, government policies on tackling social exclusion may have more relevance than further changes in legislation affecting homelessness or housing allocations which can do no more than juggle with who gets the more and less attractive houses. As Chris Holmes (Director of Shelter) has put it, housing allocations 'need to be seen as one key component in a far broader approach towards community regeneration, which include high quality management of services, investment in physical and environmental improvements and creating work opportunities' (Holmes 1998, p.11). There are, as yet, many initiatives but no simple answers in the area of estate regeneration and building sustainable communities. Two points are relevant here.

First, while it is important not to ascribe too much significance to housing allocation issues, they do undoubtedly have a role to play in seeking to avoid (or reduce) the processes of social segregation which create highly deprived communities. Some authorities and housing associations have developed local lettings policies with this in mind (Griffiths *et al.* 1996). It is perhaps in this context, too, that contentious policies of excluding 'anti-social' applicants from the Housing Register (and thus from social rented housing) should be viewed. While not always new, policies to exclude applicants with outstanding rent arrears or a history of anti-social behaviour or violence have achieved a higher profile since the Housing Act 1996 (Blake 1997).

Exclusions of this kind were apparently condoned by the draft Code of Guidance issued by the Departments of the Environment and Health to assist local authorities in implementing the new legislation (Department of Environment – Department of Health 1996). The rationale for exclusions on grounds of anti-social behaviour lies in desires to control or improve social problems on council estates by not housing the potentially most difficult and disruptive tenants. Homeless families should not be affected by such exclusions (since they have a statutory right to appear on the Register), though this could be problematic where authorities are seeking to maximise rehousing from the Register without treating applicants through formal homelessness channels. The effects of exclusions should be monitored, although it is not clear that authorities have actually set up systems to do so.

Second, there is a widespread realisation that local housing authorities will not be able to tackle estate regeneration alone, through physical improvements and housing management initiatives. There is a new emphasis on bringing together different agencies in the statutory and voluntary sectors who, together with the local community, will form more or less formal partnerships for holistic regeneration. For example, local service partnerships have been developed in Burnley and Coventry involving the local authorities (housing, social services, education, leisure services and others), health authorities, education colleges and voluntary organisations which have influenced the targeting of resources and sought to improve local service provision (Gregory 1998).

Again housing associations are increasingly looking to form and take part in partnerships to try to build communities on their estates (Clapham and Evans 1998). The Department of the Environment, Transport and the Regions (which has main responsibility for housing) is commissioning the preparation of good practice guidance for local authorities on estate regeneration which will no doubt refer to these and other examples. The Government's New Deal for Communities and the work of the Social Exclusion Unit will be very relevant over the next few years.

Conclusion

This chapter has described the development of homelessness legislation in England and Wales up to and including the Housing Act 1996. It has noted that families with children are a relatively favoured group within this legislation, and that for them it has provided an important channel to social rented housing.

While rights for homeless people were reduced by the 1996 Act, practical effects in terms of outcomes may not differ that much from the previous regime, although this could depend on how local authorities choose to exercise their discretion in implementing the Act.

For the future, any further legislative change may be less important than ensuring that improvements continue in the quality of service being offered to homeless families and the ways in which they are treated. Quite as important, there must be links between homelessness policies and practices and efforts to improve and regenerate problematic social rented housing. Increasingly, those involved in the health and well-being of children must seriously consider what is needed after the offer of accommodation to create a home. This will involve increasing partnership between housing, social services and health staff, with others, in attempts to build communities on estates where people want to live.

CHAPTER 9

The Impact of Health and Social Services

Stuart Cumella

Need and access

Previous chapters have shown that homeless families are a high risk group
for both general and mental health disorders, which are often exacerbated by
poor quality temporary accommodation and difficulties in accessing health
and social care. This chapter reviews previous research on the impact of
health and social care services on homeless families, and summarises relevant
results from the Birmingham Survey of Families in Homeless Centres out-
lined in Chapter 2.

Studies of homeless families in England have found that about 95 per cent
are registered with a general practitioner. This is often a temporary
registration with a practice near their homeless centre or current accommodation, although some families remain registered with the practice they
had used before they became homeless and travel several miles to see a GP.
(Conway 1988; Victor 1992; Connelly and Crown 1994). The majority of
facilities for homeless families probably have some contact with health
visitors (Drennan and Stearn 1986), who monitor the health of children
below the age of five years.

Problems of access to primary healthcare among homeless families may
account in part for their high rates of contact with hospital accident and
emergency departments (Victor 1992; Lissauer *et al.* 1993). One study in
London found that ten per cent of paediatric beds were occupied by children
from homeless families (Victor *et al.* 1989). Another found that homeless
children were twice as likely to be admitted to hospital as children in

permanent housing, with particularly high admission rates for accidents and infectious diseases. (Lissauer *et al.* 1993).

Refugees form a substantial minority of homeless families in some London boroughs, and this group have particularly poor access to primary healthcare, as well as lower rates of immunisations and other preventive health procedures (Brooks and Patel 1995). Greater dependence on hospital-based services among homeless families has also been reported in the USA, where the majority of such families have no regular source of primary healthcare (Alperstein, Rappaport and Flanigan 1988; Miller and Lin 1988; Hu *et al.* 1989; Parker *et al.* 1991).

There is no information available from previous research about rates of contact among homeless families in England with specialist mental health services. There are some descriptions of specialist mental health services for single homeless people (see for example Ferguson and Dixon 1992; Commander, Odell and Sashidharan 1997), but none of services specifically targeted at homeless families. However, there is one report of a drop-in clinic in London providing play sessions for young children and advice for parents (Hammond and Bell 1995). Rather more information is available from US research, which has found that despite high levels of psychiatric morbidity among mothers and children in homeless families, few appear to have received appropriate treatment or have had contact with specialist services (Miller and Lin 1988; Zima, Wells and Freeman 1994; Zima *et al.* 1996; Buckner and Bassuk 1997).

Studies in the USA have likewise found lower rates of contact with welfare agencies and income support schemes among homeless families than among other low-income families (Bassuk and Rosenberg 1988). In cases where homeless families are in contact with welfare agencies, these tend to follow referral of children at risk of abuse (Bassuk, Rubin and Lauriat 1986). There have been no comparable studies of homeless families' contacts with social services in England, although a review of social work practice with homeless families found that some social services departments had specialist teams for this group of people. These aimed to prevent children being admitted to care, by counselling families in temporary accommodation and promoting improved daycare facilities. Social workers in the teams tended to regard children in homeless accommodation as at risk of neglect more than abuse, because of the absence of men (and hence of abusers) in many homeless facilities, and the difficulty of concealing abuse in crowded accommodation (Stewart and Stewart 1992).

Lack of residential stability is associated with loss of schooling (Bassuk and Rosenburg 1988; Wood *et al.* 1990), but there may be several reasons preventing continuity of education. A survey of head teachers and families in England identified fear of domestic violence and lack of financial support for transport as key factors, but noted that homeless families also encountered obstacles in registering children for new schools because of waiting lists, delays in authorising free school meals, and practical problems such as having to buy a new school uniform. These problems were even more prominent for large families and those seeking places for children with special needs (Power, Whitty and Youdell 1995).

The Birmingham Study
Contacts with services before becoming homeless

Further information about contacts by homeless families with health and social services is available from the Birmingham study described in Chapter 2. Respondents in both the homeless and comparison samples were presented with a checklist of health and social services, and asked to record those contacted at least once during the preceding year, for each adult and child in the household.

The interview schedule did not request reasons for contacts, although this information was volunteered by most respondents. Similar questions were included in the follow-up interviews, although respondents in the homeless sample were also asked to distinguish between contacts when in the homeless centre and since rehousing. It was not practicable to check parental reports of contacts with agency records, and the results presented here may therefore differ from the true rate.

Table 9.1 shows the proportion of parents and children in both samples who had been in contact with health and social services at some time during the preceding year, according to parental reports. As noted in Chapter 2, three-quarters of homeless families moved directly from stable housing into a homeless centre, while the median time in temporary accommodation for the remainder was only six weeks. This means that the data in the table relates mainly to the time before they became homeless. It is therefore not surprising to find that the two samples reported broadly similar rates of contact with health and welfare services.

Over four-fifths of adults and children in both samples reported that they had seen their GP, and over half that they had visited a dentist (although less children in the homeless sample were reported to have seen one). Reported rates of contact with hospital outpatients (about a fifth in both samples) were also similar. However, parents in homeless families had significantly higher reported rates of contact with social workers, while children in these families were more likely to have been in contact with social workers and health visitors, and to have been inpatients.

Table 9.1: Contacts with health and social services during the year before families became homeless

Service	Homeless families	Comparison sample	Significance levels (not multiple comparisons)
Parental contact	(N=113)	(N=29)	
GP	84%	89%	NS
Dentist	52%	59%	NS
Outpatient	24%	15%	NS
Inpatient	17%	4%	NS
Psychiatrist	11%	0%	NS
CPN	4%	0%	NS
Social worker	31%	7%	FET: p<0.05
Child contact	(N=251)	(N=81)	
GP	83%	86%	NS
Dentist	70%	84%	FET: p<0.05
Health visitor	12%	3%	FET: p<0.05
Outpatient	20%	21%	NS
Inpatient	10%	0%	FET: p<0.01
Psychiatrist	2%	0%	NS
Educational psychologist	6%	3%	NS
Educational Welfare	2%	3%	NS
Social worker	22%	0%	FET: p<0.001

Note: FET = Fisher's Exact Test

Some of this variation can be explained by the circumstances that led to homelessness. The high rates of contact with social workers (31% of homeless parents compared with 7% of parents in the comparison sample) were associated with parental reports that their children had been abused or at risk of abuse (Fisher's Exact Test <0.001). Reasons given by parents for the inpatient admission of their children during the year before the interview indicated that about half followed asthmatic attacks. This suggests a possibility that some children may have developed psychosomatic disorders in response to a disrupted home environment, or that hospital admission may have resulted from raised levels of anxiety among their parents. However, this issue clearly requires further investigation.

Few parents or children in either sample had reported contact with specialist mental health services. Eleven per cent of parents in the homeless sample reported that they had seen a psychiatrist, and four per cent that they had seen a community psychiatric nurse (CPN). Among children in the homeless sample, two per cent were reported to have been in contact with a psychiatrist, and six per cent with an educational psychologist. Among children above the clinical cut-off on the Child Behaviour Checklist (CBCL), six per cent had been in contact with a psychiatrist, and thirteen per cent with an educational psychologist.

Contacts with services when in homeless centres

As noted in Chapter 2, most families in the homeless sample had been in a homeless centre for a comparatively brief period (median = 8 weeks, quartiles = 4–12 weeks). During this time, a majority of the parents were in contact with a GP (61%), and over a third (35%) with a social worker. Reported contact rates among children while in homeless centres were lower, at 30 per cent for a GP and 32 per cent for a social worker.

Before becoming homeless, 73 per cent of the children in the sample of homeless families had been attending mainstream school, two per cent in a special school, 13 per cent in nursery schools, while 12 per cent were below school age and had not attended nursery provision. At the initial interviews, the proportion in mainstream schools had fallen to 29 per cent, the proportion in special schools to one per cent, and the proportion in nursery education to five per cent. Some children had ceased attending their old school because of the distance involved, the problems meeting transport costs, and a fear that violent partners would follow the children from the school to the homeless centre.

Parents were often reluctant to register their children for a new school because they believed it would be disruptive to transfer them to one school near the homeless centre and a second school when they were rehoused in another area. Some parents reported that they had difficulty registering their children for schools and nursery schools because schools close to the homeless centres did not have vacancies. For many children, the change of school or the lack of school meant the disruption of social networks and friendships at a time when their home life was in crisis. The impact of a change of school is shown in the following report by a seven-year-old girl:

> I'm at a new school now. I travel a long way. I have to get two buses. I don't like it because it makes me sick. I think it's a better school. We do writing, history, and English, but I miss my friends. There's nobody to talk to, so I just walk around on my own.

Services contacts after leaving homeless centre

By the follow-up interviews, nine out of ten (90%) children in the homeless families were attending school, including seven per cent in nursery school, 82 per cent in mainstream school, and one per cent in special school. These figures are almost identical to those among the comparison sample, in which 89 per cent attended school, but it is notable that both samples included a small number of children of school age who were not attending any school.

Among those attending school, 29 per cent had returned to the same school they attended before becoming homeless, while the remaining 71 per cent were at different schools. Some children (32%) had attended two or more schools during the year since they became homeless. According to parental reports, almost half (47%) of the children of school age had not lost any weeks schooling because of homelessness. For those who did lose schooling, the median number of weeks lost was ten. Parents reported that ten per cent of children had received special lessons to help them catch up with work lost.

Table 9.2 compares rates of contact after becoming homeless (including both time spent in homeless centres and after) with rates over the equivalent period among the comparison sample. A high proportion of mothers and children in both samples saw their GP at least once, with a significant minority also in contact with outpatient services. There were statistically significant differences between the samples in contacts with three professional services. Mothers and children in the homeless sample had less contacts with dentists, presumably as a result of difficulties they encountered in registering with a new dentist at a time when many dentists were leaving the National Health Service.

A higher proportion of children in homeless families were in contact with a health visitor (26% of those under school age, compared with 3% among children in the comparison sample). Rates of contact with hospital outpatient services were high in both samples, being typical of low income families in central urban areas (Spencer 1993), but there was no statistically significant difference between the samples in reported inpatient admissions.

Table 9.2: Contacts with health and social services between initial and follow-up interviews

Service	Homeless families	Comparison sample	Significance levels (not multiple comparisons)
Parental contact	(N=41)	(N=21)	
GP	98%	91%	NS
Dentist	40%	80%	FET: p<0.01
Outpatient	33%	15%	NS
Inpatient	13%	0%	NS
Psychiatrist	13%	0%	NS
CPN	8%	0%	NS
Social worker	45%	0%	FET: p<0.01
Child contact	(N=103)	(N=54)	
GP	87%	80%	NS
Dentist	50%	85%	FET: p<0.001
Health visitor	15%	2%	FET: p<0.001
Outpatient	18%	26%	NS
Inpatient	1%	0%	NS
Psychiatrist	5%	0%	NS
Educational psychologist	4%	0%	NS
Educational Welfare	5%	0%	NS
Social worker	36%	0%	FET: p<0.001

The most marked difference between the samples occurred in reported contacts with social services. Over a third (36%) of children in the homeless families but none of the comparison sample saw a social worker during the year between the two interviews. According to parental reports only six per cent of children in the homeless sample remained on the at risk register, two per cent had been in care ('looked after by the local authority') since becoming homeless, but none had been the subject of abuse.

Contacts with specialist mental health services continued to be low for both mothers and children in the homeless sample despite the high prevalence of psychiatric morbidity both immediately after becoming homeless and at the follow-up interviews. Thirteen per cent of mothers and five per cent of children had seen a psychiatrist and eight per cent of parents had seen a CPN. These rates were similar to those during the year before admission to the homeless centre. Four per cent of children in the homeless sample were in contact with an educational psychologist during the year before the follow-up interviews.

Implications

The interpretation of the results reported in this chapter should take account of the response rate in the research, and the possibility that non-respondents differed in some respects from those who were interviewed. The comparison sample is small, so any comparisons between the two samples have low power. Nevertheless, the results confirm earlier research with homeless families, which show that the great majority are able to access primary healthcare services, in contrast with the problems experienced by many single homeless people (Fisher and Collins 1993). Contact rates were also high for social workers, indicating that the social services department was effective in maintaining contact with children who had been abused or were otherwise deemed at risk. Greater problems were encountered by homeless families in maintaining continuity of education and access to mental health services.

An immediate consequence of homelessness for most children was loss of schooling, and hence of the psychological protection this can provide for a child through friendships, continuity of routine, and an opportunity to achieve despite adversity in family life. Few children or parents appear to have received any specialist help to enable them to manage this transition, or their recent experience of loss of home, coupled in many cases with family disintegration, physical or sexual abuse, domestic and neighbourhood violence, developmental delay, or parental mental illness. This confirms the findings of several reviews of child and adolescent mental health services in England, which have found them to be generally unresponsive to emergencies, poorly matched to need, and fragmented between the NHS, education authorities, and social services departments (Kurtz, Thornes and Wolkind 1994; Williams and Richardson 1995).

The multiple problems experienced by children in homeless families and the possibility that the experience of homelessness will itself intensify these problems indicates a need for systemic change at both agency and practitioner levels. This should include:

- *The continuation of schooling for children in homeless centres.* Local education authorities should aim to maintain school attendance among children in homeless families by ensuring that schools and nursery schools near homeless centres have places designated for such children, by minimising delays in admission, and by ensuring that the formula for funding the local management of schools does not disadvantage schools with a high turnover of pupils.

- *The provision of designated treatment services for homeless families.* Health authorities and local authorities should ensure that homeless families are a high priority for rapid assessment and treatment by paediatric and mental health services. This need can probably be met most effectively by designated sessions for paediatricians, psychiatrists, educational psychologists, health visitors and community nurses. Clinicians with a special responsibility for work with homeless families should aim to build links with the schools and primary care teams used by families in homeless centres, and train staff in homeless centres to identify signs of psychiatric disorders in parents and children and ensure appropriate referrals.

- *Systemic change in local operating procedures.* There is need for each homeless centre to become part of a network of local health, education, and social services, to ensure rapid referral, information exchange, and access to routine immunisations and health checks. Networks can be facilitated by the attachment of a health visitor and social worker to each homeless centre.

CHAPTER 10

Homeless Children

Public Health Perspectives

Christina R. Victor

Introduction

The term 'homelessness' is used rather homogeneously, as if homeless people were a single social group characterised by a single set of health needs which could be met by a universal policy response. However, the homeless population is actually heterogeneous, for within its ambit are a range of different circumstances and populations. Included within this term are those who are without any form of accommodation and who are 'sleeping rough', those who are accepted as being 'legally homeless', and those living in concealed households or other 'fragile' housing arrangements. In this book we are concerned with the legal or official homeless population group, as it is within this segment of the homeless population that children are found. In this chapter, from a public health perspective, we summarise the research describing the numbers of children who are homeless, examine the health needs presented by this population, describe the literature describing their use of services and speculate upon the types of services and modes of delivery most appropriate for this population.

How many homeless children are there?

In 1994 approximately 287,000 households applied to the local authority, of which 143,500 were accepted as homeless (see Victor 1997 for a review of trends in homelessness). It is interesting to speculate upon what became of those who were unsuccessful in their application. This figure of 143,500 is almost certainly a significant underestimate, both because of the limitations imposed by the qualifying criteria (i.e. not making themselves intentionally homeless, fitting within one of the priority need categories and having a local connection with the area in which they are seeking rehousing) but also because of the discretion with which these criteria are applied.

To determine the need for health care demonstrated by homeless children (or indeed any other population sub-group), it is important to enumerate the size of the population. Published data concerning the numbers of homeless people relate only to the total numbers of households accepted and the reasons why households were successful. They provide no insight into the nature and characteristics of this population. This makes estimating the number of homeless children, either locally or nationally, problematic. Analysis of the reasons why households are accepted as homeless demonstrates that 12 per cent of households were accepted because of pregnancy, and 60 per cent because the household contained dependent children (those aged 0 to 16).

From this we can estimate that 72 per cent (103,320) homeless households contained children. This is remarkably similar to the proportion of families with dependent children reported in Northwest Thames (65% of a sample of those living in temporary accommodation (Victor 1996)) and in a national sample (67% (Gill *et al.* 1996)). However, this does not provide insight into either the number or ages of children within these households, nor any other information about the composition of the family. For these estimates we must use evidence provided by local surveys to illustrate the potential number of homeless children. It is estimated that the mean household size for the homeless population is 2.3, giving a total family size of 330,505. Victor (1996) reports that of those 65 per cent of households with dependent children, the mean number of children was 1.7. Application of these estimates to national data suggests that there are 175,644 homeless children in Britain, of which the vast majority (67%) are pre-school age; and 26 per cent in the primary school age group (5 to 10) (Victor 1996). About one-third (38%) of these children will be living in single parent families. These data may be used to estimate the number of homeless children for specific geographical areas.

In additional there are young people (who could well fall within the term 'children') within the other segments of the homeless population. It is estimated that about one per cent of those sleeping rough are aged under 20, and that 13 per cent of hostel dwellers are also within this age group. Using estimates from Victor (1997) for the size of these two populations (rough sleepers between 3000 and 6000, and hostel dwellers between 19,417 and

50,000), this represents 2294 to 7100 potentially vulnerable teenagers living in homeless circumstances. Furthermore, two per cent of the official homeless households are headed by a person aged 16 to 19. The health needs of older teenagers, and the most effective ways to meet these, should not be ignored because of our concerns for the very young children who are born into homelessness or who experience it at a young age.

The health of homeless children

Determining the heath needs of homeless children is a prerequisite for the development, implementation and establishment of the appropriate style and configuration of health services. However, there are profound methodological problems in systematically enumerating these needs. As already indicated in this chapter (and elsewhere in the book), there are considerable difficulties in defining which circumstances determine homelessness. Even for infants and pre-school children there are no readily available lists identifying homeless children which could form the sampling frame for a systematic survey. Similarly, for children of school age, educational authorities (or indeed schools) may not necessarily be aware of those on the roll that are homeless (Amery, Tomkins and Victor 1995). Consequently, a popular approach is to study a sample of homeless children attending specialist or generic services. However, as the survey of paediatric clinic attendees by Richman *et al.* (1991) shows, this is subject to selection bias because those who use services may not be representative of the total population.

For example, paediatric walk-in clinic users could be sicker than non-users (or indeed the opposite may be the case). We may conclude only that the sample of service users is biased; we cannot determine the direction of the bias, and this makes generalising from the results problematic. A different approach is to try to enumerate the total homeless population and then determine the health needs of the group (see for example the national survey of psychiatric morbidity (Gill *et al.* 1996) or more local studies (Whynes and Giggs 1992)). However, the problem of accurately establishing the number of homeless children (or indeed adults) in an area also means that it is difficult, if not impossible, to calculate utilisation rates for services and to make comparisons with local (and national) populations.

Having identified a population to study, there are further problems to be overcome. The most robust studies are those based upon the use of standardised data collection instruments for which population norms (or data derived from an appropriate comparison group) are available. However, studies are often retrospective in nature, and based upon case note review (Richman *et al.* 1991) or the use of non-standardised questions/instruments. Furthermore, there are challenging issues in the use of comparison groups. Much of the early work in the area of homelessness and health was content simply to 'describe' or 'present' the health of homeless children (see for example Drennan and Stern 1986; Lovell 1986). However, it is insufficient to let the results of any health survey 'speak for them'; the results of surveys of health and homeless people need to be placed in context. Studies should seek to determine the additional health deficits resulting from homelessness (that is those over and above any health deficits resulting from poverty or poor social networks).

Hence, we need to make comparisons with an appropriate population. This should be age-sex matched but also needs to take into account the degree of disadvantage represented. Simply comparing homeless people with another disadvantaged group will underestimate the 'true' negative outcomes from homelessness. For example we should be comparing the percentage of low birth weight babies amongst homeless mothers, not with the percentage from Tower Hamlets or Paddington but with more affluent areas such as Guildford.

Study design is the final methodological issue that must be considered. Many studies are retrospective in nature. They may have become out-of-date and no longer reflect the current picture. Furthermore, other studies are usually cross-sectional studies based upon the situation at one point in time. In such studies, estimates can be provided as to the prevalence of accidents or asthma amongst homeless children of different ages. However, this study design does not take into account the amount of time families may have been homeless. Does the prevalence of health problems increase with the amount of time spent as homeless and/or the ages at which children experience homelessness? Does the number/severity of problems increase arithmetically or exponentially? Most important, we cannot be certain that the negative health effects observed are ameliorated once the family is housed. Does housing reduce (but not eradicate) problems? Our knowledge about the health of homeless children is far from perfect and often based upon rather weak descriptive evidence. Clearly, there is an extensive research agenda which requires attention.

Given these *caveats*, what do we know about the health needs of homeless children? This information is essential to any development of appropriate services. If we do not determine the nature and extent of the major health problems of homeless children, we are in danger of developing inappropriate (or incorrect) service responses. These have been indicated in detail in Chapters 3 and 4. However, it is worth reiterating that there is consistent, if not scientifically robust, descriptive evidence for an elevated prevalence and incidence of low birth weight, developmental delay, chronic health problems (such as asthma), infections and infectious diseases and accidents in homeless children. The occurrence of psychological and behavioural problems is also elevated in this population. Parents, when interviewed, are in no doubt that living in temporary accommodation (such as private sector leased or bed and breakfast) is detrimental to their children's health. A survey conducted in Oxford reported that 47 per cent of a small sample of parents felt that their children's health had deteriorated since living in bed and breakfast accommodation (Vickers 1991). The variety of problems presented by homeless children indicate that this population requires access to appropriate services in both the primary and secondary areas of health service provision, as well as access to preventive health services.

Use of health services

Research has examined the use made by homeless families of both primary and secondary care services. One problem in many studies is that data are not always presented (or collected) separately for children as distinct from other members of the households. Hence, published research may significantly under- (or over-) estimate the use of services made by homeless people.

Bearing in mind these difficulties, studies from London and elsewhere have reported extensive use of primary and secondary health care services by homeless families (see for example Pleace and Quilgars 1996 and Chapter 9 in this volume). These data demonstrate consistently that in specific localities homeless families can comprise a significant element of services' workload. For example, several surveys from St Mary's indicated that homeless children represented 20 per cent of paediatric admissions and 15 per cent of users of a paediatric walk-in clinic (Richman et al. 1991). For children admitted as inpatients, assuming an average length of stay, this can represent a significant financial cost.

Given the apparently high rates of service use by homeless children and their families, especially when making comparisons with local populations, it would be easy to conclude that all their health care needs were being adequately met. However, if we calculate standardised rates of service use (*which correct* for the very distinct demographic profile of the homeless population), then the situation appears to suggest extensive unmet needs. For example, in the survey undertaken of bed and breakfast accommodation for homeless people in Paddington, four per cent of the sample had seen a health visitor in the previous 14 days, compared with 15 per cent of the regional population. However, if we take into account the differing age structure of the two groups then the standardised utilisation rate for homeless people is 93 per cent, that is they are less likely to receive this service than regional residents of the same age (Victor 1996). If this rate had been standardised to take into account the greater number of pre-school children in the population, then it is likely that this differential would have been even greater.

Access to primary care is a persistent issue for those concerned with the provision of services to homeless families and children. A consistent explanation for the apparently high use of casualty departments and other emergency clinics has been that such services are used as substitutes for primary care services, access to which is being denied (or made difficult) for homeless families. Whilst we should not underestimate the barriers to accessing care which homeless families can face, these probably derive from more subtle and complex causes than an overt refusal to register such families. Indeed it has been shown that about 95 per cent of the 'official' homeless population are registered with a GP (Gill *et al.* 1996; Victor 1996).

From this it possible to conclude that homeless families have easy access to primary care. However, the situation is more complex than these optimistic data might suggest. Because of the very common practice of locating homeless families in temporary accommodation outside their area of origin, the GP could be some distance from where the family is living. Hence, the practice (rather than theory) of accessing primary care is more problematic. Obtaining temporary registration in districts characterised by large concentrations of homeless people can be hard. The practicalities of using such services may be difficult without some local knowledge (e.g. bus routes) and in situations where families have reduced access to informal social support and few financial resources. Such problems can be accentuated in many inner city areas where the infrastructure of primary care may be much less developed. Consequently, residents of inner city districts, regardless of housing status, use secondary services (especially accident and emergency) as a substitute for difficult-to-obtain primary care.

Hence, from the perspective of the homeless family (but not of the service providers), it might be more appropriate to seek health care from services which are close by, such as casualty departments of major hospitals. The survey described by Richman *et al.* (1991) attempted to investigate why parents had brought their child to the paediatric walk-in clinic rather than consulting their GP. The responses provided by parents centred upon the perceived accessibility of the clinic (in comparison with the local primary care) and the quality of service provided by the clinic. This example indicates that, though many have been prepared to judge that homeless people use the secondary care sector inappropriately, there has been comparatively little research into the types and styles of services which homeless people would like to see developed.

Discussion

There are significant numbers of homeless children in Britain. Most of these are covered by the legal definition of homelessness. By employing data from local surveys we can estimate the number of pre- and school-age homeless children either nationally or locally. Furthermore, we can describe a consistent pattern of health needs which are presented by this population. Providing solutions as to the most appropriate method of responding to these needs is more problematic. In developing services for homeless children there are considerable practical difficulties. The mobility of this population must be acknowledged. Cross-sectional surveys provide only a partial insight into the mobility of this group, as any such approach will over-represent the long-stayers. Victor (1996) reports that 23 per cent of her sample had been in their current bed and breakfast for one month or less.

Whilst it is true that some families appear to become marooned in particular hotels, the majority of this population is highly mobile. Developing services that can respond to such fluidity and provide continuity of care in the absence of medical records and notes is challenging. Not only are the people concerned highly mobile but so are the forms of temporary accommodation such families may use prior to permanent rehousing. The peak in use of bed and breakfast hotels has probably passed. However, it is often difficult to track the changing nature and identity of this temporary accommodation and in the absence of accurate and comprehensive lists it is difficult to identify the whereabouts of homeless people.

There have been many attempts to develop specialist services for homeless families (see Pleace and Quilgars (1996) for a description of a variety of these initiatives). Many districts have developed specialist outreach health visitors dedicated to the care of homeless families. However, as noted above, there are considerable problems involved in finding the temporary accommodation used and the families themselves. Many of these services have been described but few have been rigorously evaluated. Consequently, we do not have robust evidence as to which style of service delivery, specialist or generic, produces the best outcome for homeless people. There is considerable need for good evaluative studies that compare the different models of care. In particular, we need to move beyond qualitative description of a service to establishing scientific evidence on which to base our decisions.

We need to look at services for homeless families and children across all six of the Maxwell criteria (Maxwell 1984). This means we need to investigate not simply effectiveness, efficiency and equity, but also accessibility, appropriateness and acceptability. We must pay more attention to including homeless families in our research to present their views, especially on acceptability, appropriateness and accessibility. One theoretical illustration of this might be the use of primary care by homeless families. Instead of trying to ignore the expressed demands and wishes of homeless people and trying to divert them to less appropriate and primary care, perhaps we would be better served by developing more accessible 'primary care' services with the accident and emergency departments. Failure to include the perspective of users will result in the development of inappropriate services which do not respond to the health needs presented. Such an approach is both inefficient and arrogant.

Key points

- The homeless population is heterogeneous in nature. The 'official' population is only one element of this group.

- Homeless children are concentrated in the official homeless population – 73 per cent of such households include children.

- The number of children within the official homeless population is estimated at 103, 000, of which 67 per cent are pre-school age.

- Descriptive cross-sectional studies consistently report a high prevalence of developmental delay, infection and infectious disease, accidents, chronic health problems (e.g. asthma), psychological and behavioural problems amongst homeless children.

- It is uncertain if such problems are ameliorated by rehousing.

- Homeless children are high users of secondary care but it is unlikely that all health service needs are being met.

- There are continuing problems with access to primary care.

- There is no clear evidence as to whether homeless children's health needs are best met by generic or specialist services.

- There is an urgent need to include homeless people's views on type and style of service delivery and models of care.

CHAPTER II

Doubly Disadvantaged
Education and the Homeless Child
Sally Power, Geoff Whitty and Deborah Youdell

Introduction

Becoming homeless represents one of the most acute forms of social loss. It is not only linked to other forms of disadvantage, such as poverty and unemployment, as other chapters in this book have illustrated, but it also compounds these disadvantages. Given the apparently intractable relationship between homelessness and disadvantage, it is perhaps not surprising that education is sometimes held up as providing the way forward. First, and in the longer term, a successful educational career potentially provides one of the few mechanisms through which the cycle of cumulative disadvantage can be broken. Second, and perhaps of more immediate importance to homeless families, the stability and support of regular attendance at school can offer a useful counterbalance to the disruption and insecurity that arises from becoming homeless and the ensuing uncertainties of living in often inadequate temporary accommodation.

That the education system currently fails to provide many children from homeless families with an escape on either a long- or short-term basis is evident from a number of studies. Research on educational achievement, particularly from the USA, shows that homeless children perform less well than their permanently housed peers. Bassuk and Rosenberg (1988) found that 40 per cent of a sample of homeless students were failing or producing below average work. One quarter were in special classes. Stronge (1992) found that homeless students scored one year below their grade level, with the deficit increasing to up to three years as they grew older. Kozol (1988) found that children living in welfare hotels were two to three grades behind their peers. In the UK, Stepien and Colleagues (1996) found that the vocabulary development of homeless children was behind that of others. These studies suggest that it is unlikely that education alone will propel homeless children towards a more advantaged future. But it would also seem that schools are frequently unable to provide even short-term respite. Studies from England (Inner London Education Authority 1987) and, more recently, the USA (Stronge 1992) show that high numbers of students are not in school at all. Stronge (1992) estimates that 43 per cent of homeless children in the USA are not attending school on a regular basis.

In this chapter we explore some of the processes that lie behind figures such as these. Our own research represents one of the few projects, at least within the UK, that attempts to explore what happens when the homeless child meets the education system. The research, funded by the British homelessness charity *Shelter*, involved a national survey of local education authorities (LEAs) and more detailed investigations with local authority professionals concerned with housing and education, schools and homeless parents and pupils, within three case study areas. The national survey of 109 LEAs elicited a response of 71 per cent. A survey of the 433 schools in the three case study areas brought a 42 per cent response rate – with over one third (71) of the schools which responded having homeless pupils on roll. In depth interviews were conducted within 12 of these schools and with parents and children from 14 homeless households. In the following sections we sketch out some of the key findings from the research and outline a number of recommendations (for more details of the research, its findings and recommendations, see Power, Whitty and Youdell 1995).

Homelessness and education provision

Finding and maintaining a school place

Many of the parents and professionals with whom we spoke talked of the difficulties they experienced in either trying to find a place at a new school or in trying to maintain a school place after they had been rehoused in temporary accommodation. Although there may be no shortage of school places across any one area, these are often unevenly distributed. One-fifth of LEAs in our survey cited oversubscription of school places as a major problem for homeless families. This was particularly acute in large urban areas – where the incidence of homelessness is usually highest. In the words of one parent: 'I went around all of the schools, they said they were full. I filled in application forms, now we are on the waiting list'. Large families found it particularly difficult to find places for all of their children in one school so that they had to use several different schools. This led to additional work finding places, staggered entry, excessive time and cost delivering and collecting children from each school, as well as a lack of sibling support.

The ability to find school places is also to some extent dependent on local knowledge – the kind of knowledge that families rehoused some way from their original home just do not have. One mother in bed and breakfast accommodation commented that she just didn't know where the local schools were. For refugees seeking political asylum the situation is compounded by lack of knowledge of the education system as a whole, and in some cases, by language difficulties.

It is perhaps the uncertainty of temporary housing that creates the most difficulties for homeless parents when they try to plan for their children's education. Some families understandably wanted to send their children to school in the area in which they expected to be permanently housed. But the lack of information about where this might be or when they could expect to be moved left them not knowing what to do. In addition, current regulations on help with transport costs meant that, even if parents did place their children at schools in anticipation of their future move, they would have to bear the financial burden themselves.

It is not surprising that in many cases parents keep their children at home – particularly where they believe they will be rehoused quickly. Unfortunately though, temporary accommodation placements are frequently not as temporary as parents may have hoped. Although in the UK the average length of stay in temporary accommodation is three months (Shelter 1994), some families may remain in such housing for many years (Greve 1991). Sharma's survey of one hundred families living in a bed and breakfast hotel (Sharma 1987) revealed that just under half of the sample had been there over six months at the time of interview. One-quarter had been there for more than one year and were likely to end up staying there much longer. Similarly, users of the Bayswater Hotel Homelessness Project reported being in bed and breakfast accommodation for up to two years (Crane 1990). The parents we spoke to might have placed their children at local schools had they known that their stay was to be more than a few weeks long, for example: 'If I'd known how long we'd be here I would have been up at the school the next day and got them straight in. Housing [officers] should be up-front, they keep building our hopes up'.

In the light of such uncertainty of where and when they would be rehoused and the desire to achieve continuity in their children's education, many parents preferred to try and maintain a place at the old school. But, certainly in the areas we researched, there was no provision to help such parents. This often meant they had to spend substantial amounts of time and their limited income on travelling — indeed one head teacher strongly discouraged families from maintaining previous school places as it led to continual lateness and absence. An additional concern for those households who had been made homeless through domestic violence was the need for safety. One teenager reported that she was repeatedly late for school as she had to take two buses in order to avoid passing her father's home each morning.

Educational progress and participation

Even when homeless children do find an available and accessible school, they can still experience difficulties with a system that is based on regular adherence to rules and routines. As the statistics cited earlier indicate, their academic progress often lags behind that of their peers in permanent accommodation. The large majority (86%) of head teachers in our survey reported that homelessness had an impact on progress. Although the causes of underachievement are complex and homelessness itself is linked to other factors related to underachievement, the trauma and dislocation of homelessness were seen to create additional difficulties.

Irregular attendance was frequently cited as an issue and made it difficult to ensure continuity of work. This was compounded by frequent school moves. Both teachers and pupils spoke of the difficulties of having to adapt to new environments and new syllabuses. For pupils living in bed and breakfast accommodation, lack of space and facilities meant they were often ill prepared for school and unable to complete homework.

In terms of social development, the constant moves meant that homeless children were often unable to form supportive relationships at school. Pupils reported: 'I don't like going into new schools, it's embarrassing. I don't know what to do, I go dead shy'; 'I don't rush into making friends'; '…half the time I didn't bother to try and mix because we would only get moved again'. This reluctance can be at least partly explained by the stigma of homelessness. Homeless pupils felt they were seen as outsiders. One mother reported that her son 'was called all sorts of names because he didn't have a house'. One girl recalled how: 'The kids knew I was moving all over. The lads were the worst; they nicknamed me "gypsy". I'd take it as a laugh at first but it would get to me'. Attempts to overcome prejudice by tackling homelessness as an issue within the curriculum tended to be sporadic and *ad hoc* and seemed to have a lower profile than similar work in the USA (see for example, Patton 1996, and Hoffbauer and Prenn 1996).

Locating responsibility

It is clear from the preceding section that whatever promise the education system might potentially hold for homeless children, it is some way from being realised. Conventional explanations for the educational difficulties encountered by homeless children often locate the shortcomings, at least implicitly, within the homeless families themselves. Indeed, some of our welfare and education professionals were quite explicit about this. A few stated that homeless families kept their children out of school intentionally – claiming that education was not valued and that older children were kept at home to help with younger children or to provide company and a sense of security. One commented that 'a lot of parents use homelessness as an excuse for not pushing their children'. However, our research provided little support for such a claim. Many parents were desperate for their children to go to school. Clearly, there were occasions when other crises connected with homelessness took priority over education, but in many cases it would appear to be the inability of the education system to cope with the needs of homeless households rather than the indifference of parents that led to absences from school. In particular, our survey of local authorities revealed a number of shortcomings within national and local policy and practice. It is these systemic and organisational attributes that we consider next.

Welfare support for homeless families

Divided responsibilities

Within Britain, policy formulation and implementation in housing and education are often characterised by divisions. Unlike in the USA, there is no legislation relating specifically to the education of homeless children that requires these divisions to be crossed. The two realms operate as distinct entities with little apparent linkage. Responsibility for discharging policies and providing services is also divided into tiers of government between which there are often divergent priorities and interests. This leads to much confusion surrounding the roles and responsibilities of the various welfare agencies with responsibility for homeless families. Liaison between education and housing officers in particular is patchy – and occasionally non-existent. Housing authorities are not obliged to inform other statutory agencies, including education departments, that a family with school-age children has been placed in temporary accommodation within their boundaries. Fewer than nine per cent of education authorities reported blanket notification procedures whereby they were kept regularly informed by their equivalent housing departments of homeless children.

Although very few LEAs received formal blanket notification relating to the presence of children within homeless households, some form of liaison between the LEA and the local housing authority was the norm rather than the exception. But the nature of this liaison was variable and predominantly informal. Its informal nature raised several issues. Whilst some respondents felt that communication was generally good, it was acknowledged that it took place at the discretion of individual workers and that not all families would be brought to the attention of the local authority. One education officer reported that they had requested such notification on a number of occasions but that 'the response to this is somewhat haphazard depending upon the importance placed on this request by an individual worker'. It would also appear that, when informal liaison does take place, it is often initiated by the housing authority and in response to some sort of crisis in the housing field, for example in connection with: '…[a] problem estate'; '…developing [a] system for "anti-social" tenants'; or, 'sending proceedings for non-payment of rent and arrears'. Although such issues are no doubt important, they do not indicate a commitment to develop systematic arrangements to facilitate the provision of support services on the basis of need.

Underestimating the extent of the problem

One finding that emerged from our survey of LEAs was that they tended to underestimate the scale of homelessness within their own areas. While only five local authorities perceived themselves as having a level of homelessness higher than that suggested by official statistics, over one-half reported incidences of homelessness *below* that level. Only a quarter of the sixteen LEAs classified as having the highest levels of homelessness saw themselves in this way. In general, respondents were more likely to see the areas in which they worked as having 'medium' or, even more significantly, 'low' levels of homelessness. This lack of awareness is evident in our inner London case study area. The area has a long history of homelessness and continues to feature as one of the worst affected areas. Housing authority officers reported that 3000 to 4000 new applications for housing would be received in a year. Yet the principal educational welfare officer asked us whether we had 'spoken to the boroughs which have a problem' and confidently asserted that 'there are not particularly high numbers of homeless families in this borough'.

The implications of this underestimation are difficult to establish. However, it is reasonable to suggest that if LEAs do not see homelessness as a pressing problem in their area, they are less likely to make attempts to monitor its incidence. Fifty-five LEAs (79%) reported that they kept no records – an omission that is likely to limit severely their ability to put in place policies and practices to help homeless households.

Inadequate welfare support

In those LEAs that are aware of the problem, financial and welfare support is usually provided on an *ad hoc*, discretionary or informal basis. The existence and scope of LEA policies designed to help homeless pupils and the schools they attend were highly variable. There was certainly no common practice of assigning responsibility for the education of homeless children to a particular person or office. Twenty-seven, or 39 per cent, of the 70 LEAs reported that they made some form of support available to help homeless pupils. Although LEAs with a perceived high incidence were more likely to make such provision, this should not be taken to indicate that services were provided where they were badly needed. Nearly half of those LEAs which identified themselves as having a high level of homelessness made no special provision of any kind.

Only a small minority of LEAs said they provided additional funding to schools to take account of the effects of homelessness. Seven reported funding that was distributed according to an element within the formula designed to allocate the school budget. But most were more likely to make other forms of support available. Over one-third of LEAs (24 out of 70), including three of those also providing additional funding, reported that they had some form of welfare provision which would assist homeless pupils. This included help with school uniform and free school meals and assistance in gaining admissions to schools. But while such help is obviously better than none at all, it is inconsistently distributed and can often be the first to disappear at times of financial stringency.

Additional funding provided on a systematic basis is needed not just to help individual families but also the schools they attend. The evidence from our school questionnaire and interviews shows that those schools with significant numbers of homeless pupils carry extra burdens. Indeed, some head teachers claimed that the presence of homeless children affected the educational progress of other classmates. Particularly important here is the relationship between homelessness and high pupil turnover rates. But there are also other organisational problems. One of these is extra administration. Liaison with other welfare agencies is time-consuming. Identifying and maintaining contact with homeless families is often difficult. Again, pastoral systems in schools with many homeless parents can be put under considerable strain, for which there are inadequate extra resources.

The implications of welfare restructuring

Over the last fifteen years, Britain, along with many other countries, has set about restructuring its welfare system. In both housing and education, successive reforms have been put in place that have implications for the ability of homeless households to obtain adequate education provision. On the housing front, the Thatcher and Major governments sought to promote the role of the private sector and reduce public provision to a residual level. Most recently, and as a result of the 1996 Housing Act, homeless people now have reduced housing entitlements and a diminishing chance of obtaining secure social housing. The current preference for using private rented sector accommodation is likely to be particularly damaging for homeless households, as it is often more suited to the needs of single, working and mobile people rather than families with young children (Shelter Policy Unit 1997).

On the education front, breaking the LEA 'monopoly' was a key objective of Conservative education policy. This has been done through measures designed to enhance parental choice of school while at the same time transferring responsibilities from LEAs to individual schools (see Whitty, Power and Halpin 1998). Local Management of Schools (LMS) has given schools control over their own budgets. Although the education authorities are able to retain a small amount of the budget for central services, 85 per cent is devolved to individual schools, largely on the basis of pupil numbers. This has severely limited the extent to which LEAs can pursue policies and earmark funding to counter disadvantage – such as homelessness – on an authority-wide basis.

Meanwhile, in a climate of growing competition between schools, the publication of performance indicators has made some pupils appear more of a liability than others (see Gewirtz, Ball and Bowe 1995). Some schools, especially grant maintained schools that have opted out of their LEAs, have control over their own admissions. Homeless children are often poor achievers and attenders for a variety of reasons. It would not be that surprising if schools became increasingly discriminatory in their enrolment practices. This must be a matter of major concern when we know that many homeless children already experience serious difficulties in gaining access to schools and then find themselves ill-served by the routines and priorities of institutions designed to meet the needs of a largely stable pupil population. Although there are signs that the new Labour administration intends to give a greater role to LEAs, the overall shift of responsibility to schools and the emphasis on parental choice looks set to continue (DfEE 1997). Unless proper safeguards are put in place, the plight of homeless children may not be significantly improved.

Recommendations

Housing policy and practice

There is little doubt that many of the problems which have emerged in the course of this research would be mitigated if homeless households were not placed in temporary accommodation. In the meantime, the ways in which temporary accommodation is used for housing homeless families should be reviewed. Different types of temporary accommodation can have different implications for the education of homeless pupils. Some approaches to the provision of accommodation for homeless families make it especially diffi-cult for their children to make the best use of the educational services on offer. The security, quality and location of the temporary accommodation offered are particularly important for families with school-age children. Attention should therefore be given to the following issues:

- *Length of tenure.* Where there is a need to provide temporary accommodation, it should provide families with as much stability as possible. Some of the difficulties faced by homeless families in making provision for the education of their children arose from constant uncertainty about their future housing arrangements. Families allocated temporary accommodation should be given a realistic indication of how long they are likely to have to wait for permanent rehousing.

- *Bed and breakfast hotels.* These are the most notorious form of tem-porary accommodation and clearly have a number of detrimental effects on pupils. These include overcrowding, lack of play space or homework facilities and difficulties in communication between parents and schools. The evidence from this study reinforces the case for discontinuing the use of this type of accommodation.

- *Private sector rented accommodation.* Providing it is adequate in size and condition, private sector leasehold property can provide more stability and privacy. However, children living in bed and breakfast hotels, hostels, homeless units and refuges had better contact with a range of statutory and voluntary support services than those living in private sector leasehold accommodation. Schools should therefore be made aware that such provision is also short-term and has associated difficulties for families and pupils.

- *Liaison with LEAs and schools.* Housing authorities should be required to notify other agencies, including the relevant LEAs, about all placements of homeless families and maintain close liaison with responsible professionals in the education service.

- *Out-of-area placements.* It is also clear from the research that out-of-area placements can have particularly adverse consequences for the education of homeless children. Wherever possible, homeless households with children of school age should be given priority when allocating any available accommodation near their previous residence.

Education policy and practice

It would be too simple to suggest that education can overcome the kind of disadvantages that are compounded by homelessness. However, the introduction of changes in education policy and practice could help to provide more genuinely equal educational opportunities for homeless children. On the basis of the research, we make the following recommendations:

- *Monitoring.* Education authorities should monitor the overall incidence and distribution of children living in temporary accommodation attending or requiring admission to schools. This will enable them to target resources and services more effectively.

- *Central services.* All education authorities should identify an officer as having key responsibility for the education of homeless children. This will facilitate liaison between different departments and agencies in securing appropriate provision.

- *School funding.* A factor specifically related to homelessness should be included in the formula through which funds are allocated to schools in addition to any allowance already given for overall levels of social disadvantage. This formula should be sensitive to fluctuations in pupil numbers and high pupil turnover during the course of a year.

- *Financial support for families.* The criteria determining eligibility to and application procedure for financial support such as transport, school uniforms and free school meals should take account of the specific circumstances of homeless families.

- *Admissions.* LEAs and schools should adopt a flexible approach to school capacity in order to ensure the swift entry of homeless pupils to schools thus preventing periods of missed schooling.

- *Co-operation between schools.* Schools should co-operate to assist homeless families in securing the most appropriate provision. It is important that such co-operation includes *all* kinds of publicly funded schools.

- *Records.* Schools and education authorities should devise strategies to facilitate the efficient transfer of records. Prompt receipt of these is essential to both the continuity of pupils' education and the minimisation of excessive demands upon administration time and school resources.

- *Flexible learning.* Given the difficulties which homeless pupils often face with regular attendance, schools should provide them with flexible learning opportunities. This may involve teachers providing work for pupils to undertake outside school. In addition, as many homeless pupils may have nowhere to work when they are at home, schools should make sure that there are places where homeless pupils can work outside normal lesson times.

- *Pupil integration.* In order to minimise the isolation and stigmatisation experienced by homeless pupils, schools should consider the introduction of befriending schemes and other measures to involve such pupils in the life of the school.

- *Teaching about homelessness.* In order to heighten awareness and understanding, schools should cover issues relating to homelessness within the curriculum.

- *Attendance and achievement statistics.* In the compilation of statistics relating to attendance and achievement, the particular features associated with homelessness should be taken into account. This might involve retrospective authorisation of the absences of homeless pupils who have left the school due to relocation by the housing authority and the use of sensitive 'value-added' measures of school effectiveness.

To conclude, becoming homeless is a traumatic experience. The insecurity of being placed in temporary accommodation adds further disruption at a time when families need support. For children, this disruption can be particularly confusing and distressing. As we have seen, it often means losing the security and stability of school as well as home. Unless positive action is taken by *both* housing and education professionals to ensure that homeless children are given genuinely equal educational opportunities, a disrupted home life will continue to lead to a disrupted and disadvantaged school career.

CHAPTER 12

Access to Voluntary Sector Agencies

Leila Baker

Background

Internationally, social housing provision and support in the form of benefits has been cut as a result of pressures to reduce government expenditure. This has affected young people and their housing chances. Across Europe, there is a shortage of affordable accommodation for young people wishing or needing to live independently. A survey of young European people found that the main reason for not living independently was a lack of affordable housing (Eurobarometer 1997).

Young people's expectations vary internationally, with for example young people in northern European countries more likely to live independently than their contemporaries in southern Europe. This is reflected in the extent of government policies concerning the housing needs of young people, and in the extent of voluntary assistance to this group.

What is clear, however, is that internationally we have seen a growth in homelessness, with young people making up a significant proportion of this population. Estimates produced from information supplied by European Union member states suggests that between 2.3 million and 2.7 million people may be homeless over the course a year (Avramov 1995). During the 1990s, European countries have seen a growth in the number of young people who turn to hostels for accommodation. In France, for example, the number of young people aged between 18 and 25 years requiring emergency hostel accommodation increased substantially (Avramov 1995).

This chapter seeks to address the question of how young homeless people get access to services provided by voluntary agencies. The first part of the chapter sets out some background to the issue and suggests that alongside access to services, policy makers need to consider how young people can stay in touch with services and maintain their accommodation once access is secured. The second part of the chapter sets out some recent findings on the needs of young homeless people in three geographical areas.

What are voluntary agencies and why are they different?

This section begins by placing voluntary agencies working with young homeless people in the wider context and goes on to examine how young people gain access to services. To complete the picture, the section finishes by considering some of the ways in which young people can sustain services, in particular accommodation, once access has been obtained. This is an important dimension to the subject if more youth homelessness is to be prevented, and those currently homeless are to be helped in the long term.

Voluntary sector agencies provide a wide range of services to young homeless people. These include not only accommodation, but also advice, counselling and other support, training and so on. Voluntary action pre-dates state welfare provision. Traditionally, it is independent of the existing statutory services and distinct from market-led provision. Voluntary provision of accommodation and housing services has been estimated to represent about one-fifth of the sector (Joseph Rowntree Foundation 1996). The types of accommodation available through voluntary agencies typically includes: hostels, shared and self-contained supported housing, supported lodgings, adult placements, and refuges.

In many countries, great emphasis is placed on the links between housing, training and employment, with voluntary sector agencies providing specialist accommodation for this purpose. There are examples of such provision across Europe, the most well known of these being the foyer system in France which provides accommodation together with support and counselling for those seeking employment.

Today in the UK, voluntary agencies operate in a complex network of statutory and non-statutory organisations linked by formal and informal service agreements. They continue to maintain their independence, but to greater or lesser degrees depending on their role and contractual relationship to other agencies. The most important example of the contractual relationship between voluntary and statutory agencies as far as young people are concerned, lies within the Children Act 1989 (Department of Health 1989). This explicitly states that social services authorities should use the voluntary sector to help them discharge their duties to young people (1989 Children Act, Section 17, Subsection 5(a). This explicit link between voluntary action and statutory duties is the strongest indication that the government wishes the voluntary sector to assist with the discharge of specific local authority duties.

So why is the voluntary sector different from statutory services and why should this matter in the delivery of services to young homeless people? Services provided in a voluntary setting may appear more attractive to young people. This may be precisely because they are outside the statutory services, which are seen to be part of the establishment. Staff themselves may be seen as different, for example able to spend time addressing a wider range of issues with young people, than staff in statutory services. The extent and nature of their services may be less rigid (in the sense that the services are not prescribed in legislation) and therefore more responsive to the needs and wants of the young people who approach them.

However, there are difficulties with this. On the one hand, staffing in some (but by no means all) relies on volunteers or untrained staff. This can cause problems at a service delivery level, and has been known to put staff and users at risk of actual harm (Committee of Inquiry 1995). On the other hand, voluntary organisations which have adopted a more professional approach to staff recruitment are sometimes thought to have lost their flexible and independent edge. Related to this are the contracts which many agencies now forge with statutory services. These, too, can lead to a loss of flexibility.

Another crucial and historic problem with over reliance on voluntary sector welfare provision is that it offers no guarantee of producing a comprehensive set of services across a given area (Means 1997). So, for example, a young person may find themselves homeless in an area where no emergency accommodation is available and no transport is provided to enable them to reach services elsewhere. This is particularly the case in more rural areas.

Attempts have been and continue to be made to remedy these problems by developing youth homelessness strategies, involving both statutory and voluntary agencies. These address the need for a coherent set of services to meet the needs of existing homeless young people and prevent future and repeat homelessness. This strategic approach to assisting young homeless people and those who may face housing difficulties in the future is set out in the report of the National Inquiry into Preventing Youth Homelessness carried out over 1995/6 (Evans 1996).

Means of access to voluntary sector agencies

Young people obtain access to these services either directly (by self-referral) or through a third party or referral agency. In order to maximise the opportunities for young people to obtain services, it is important that both routes are open.

Self-referral is more likely to take place where a service is known and both appears and actually is accessible. This means that physical location and quality of the building in which services are delivered can affect the attitude of young people to it. Self-referral can also come about through word of mouth – where staff gradually develop a trusting atmosphere and clients return with other young people in need of the service.

The most common third party referral in this case is probably through statutory agencies, specifically housing and social services authorities as part of their implementation of the 1989 Children Act (Department of Health 1989) and 1996 Housing Act (Department of Environment 1996). There are a variety of mechanisms for achieving this. Some social services authorities have service agreements for referring clients. In the case of accommodation providers, the authority may have an arrangement to refer young people based on a quota system or they may have purchased a specific number of bedspaces for social services clients.

However the system works, there are two important issues which emerge. First, that voluntary agencies can be directly involved in the discharge of a statutory duty (under the 1989 Children Act). Second, that referral from statutory to voluntary sector needs to be balanced with the facility to refer young people back to the statutory services where necessary. As argued at the beginning of this chapter, it is not sufficient to enable young people to obtain access to voluntary services, there must also be mechanisms in place to prevent future or repeat homelessness.

One way of achieving this is to ensure that the agencies providing short- or medium-term respite from homelessness (in hostels or supported housing) are able to refer young people for rehousing in local authority or housing association homes. Similarly that young people in need of care or support can be referred to the relevant statutory agency. In addition there are some young people whose needs do not match the kinds of services which the voluntary sector is able to provide and who, therefore, need to be able to obtain access to assessment and services from statutory agencies. In many cases, however, councils and housing associations will not rehouse young people aged 16 or 17 years old and do not accept them onto their housing register (Evans

1996). This can leave some young people inappropriately housed and not in touch with the agencies best suited to meet their needs.

Third party referral is by no means restricted to statutory authorities, however. Referral may come through a wide variety of agencies, some more obvious than others. In order to prevent future and repeat homelessness, it helps to make the services known to the widest possible range of services in touch with young people – not just the more obvious ones. This includes day centres, young people's centres, schools and colleges, health services and so on.

A referral or application for services may be assessed according to criteria set down in the policies and procedures of the voluntary agency. These criteria will vary between agencies and between different types of service. One young people's advice agency, for example, describes its entry criteria in simple terms: that the young person fits the age category of 16 to 25 years (older people are seen briefly and referred on; younger people are seen at more length, given advice and if necessary referred on). They have a number of policies on behaviour but except in extreme circumstances, these will only delay access to the service rather than prevent access altogether (unpublished data collected for Baker 1997).

Access to accommodation is different. Each agency has its own entry requirements. In areas where young people's homelessness strategies are in place or where there is a demonstrated commitment to tackling youth homelessness, directories are often published which set out all the entry requirements. Entry requirements are there to serve two main functions: to enable an agency to target their service at specific groups, for example young women; and to help make the service viable in management terms, for example where insurance is given as the reason why people with previous convictions for arson are not accepted. Each agency has the ability to deliver a certain level and standard of accommodation and support and in some cases additional services. These are also set out in directories where available. This can be especially important for voluntary sector agencies where it may be less clear to the potential users what the agency is and is not able to provide.

The extent of targeting and the nature of entry requirements vary according to the type of accommodation provided. In broad terms, emergency accommodation, such as the traditional direct access hostel (sometimes known as night shelter) has tended to apply fewer criteria than, for example, the newer and generally smaller supported housing schemes.

This distinction has become less apparent as the older hostels upgrade their accommodation.

In addition to targeting a hostel or shared house at a particular group, such as young men, some accommodation providers choose to have targets for the number or proportion of residents they can take from specific groups. In some cases, this means setting aside a particular part of the building for a specific group. The clearest example of this is in direct access hostels which wish to provide a safe and secure environment for women and therefore set aside a section, annexe or other area, entry to which is restricted to women residents. A survey of direct access hostels in London found that this kind of targeting was used in connection with the needs of women, black and ethnic minority groups and lesbians and gay men (Resource Information Service 1996).

Entry requirements are also used to make a service viable and manageable. Young people may be turned away from a service because their needs differ from the services available. This is most common where a young person has care or support needs in addition to their housing need and the agency judges that it will be unable to meet those needs. (For example, people with mental health problems, alcohol and drug users and people with severe illness.) Providers may also be prevented from accepting a young person for financial reasons.

If the agency is relying on residents' benefit claims for revenue funding, then applicants who are not eligible for benefits may not be accepted. Last, providers may exclude people who have been convicted of sexual offences or arson or who are known to have a history of violence (this does not necessarily link to a conviction, see Baker 1997). The reasons for this are practical (exclusion of someone with a conviction for arson may be on insurance grounds) or to do with maintaining a harmonious resident group, especially in smaller shared houses. Young people who have been convicted of a sexual offence or arson may face increased difficulties when they leave custody. These barriers could leave some young people with no access to accommodation or support in either the statutory or voluntary sectors.

Getting and keeping accommodation in the voluntary sector

Helping young people to obtain access to voluntary sector services is not enough. Some need help staying in touch with services and managing to sustain their accommodation. All may at some stage need help to obtain a move into mainstream housing, thus (if they are leaving a voluntary sector accommodation project) making a space available for another young homeless person.

Some young people need help to sustain that accommodation. This is an important principle for the prevention of future and repeat homelessness. There are a number of ways to achieve this. Many service providers have their own integral support systems to maintain young people in their accommodation. These are delivered through key worker systems, peripatetic support staff, staffed on-site offices and so on. Typically, these have been linked directly to the provision of accommodation which has meant that when a young person moves they automatically lose the support service at the same time. In particular, the support is removed at a time of change. Recently, efforts have been made to develop models where support remains with the young person when they move. Where available, these kinds of services are instrumental in easing the transition from voluntary sector agency to mainstream housing.

For some young people with high support needs there will be ongoing support from other services, for example, social services or probation. For many, however, this will not be the case. For these and other reasons, the model of floating support has been developed. This is typically used as a mechanism for delivering support to people who need self-contained independent tenancies. Floating support is intended for tenants who are assumed to have short-term support needs. When they no longer require the support it 'floats' off to someone else. In this way, the support is not tied to any one tenancy and has the potential to reach more people. The problems with the provision of this kind of support include the fact that it is more suitable for people with short or medium term needs and this can lead to longer term needs not being addressed.

When a voluntary agency wishes to help a young person to leave their accommodation and move to more independent housing, they are faced with two problems. Where do they find new accommodation; and having found it, how do they demonstrate that the young person is ready and needs to move? There is no statutory framework for assessing whether young people are ready to move, and as a result there is no mechanism for proving that need to housing providers. Locally agreed criteria may help, but can still be subject to differences in policy and practice across the voluntary sector. The National Resettlement Project (at the National Homeless Alliance) has been developing a model which sets out stages in the resettlement process. The model aims to provide a framework for developing good quality resettlement services.

The Network Project: access to services in three areas across England

Many of the issues summarised above emerge directly from service monitoring and research in voluntary sector agencies aimed at young people. The Network Project was set up by Shelter, the National Campaign for Homeless People, in the early 1990s to undertake work to examine and improve the housing situation of young people. The Network has set up work in three contrasting areas: Lincolnshire, Crawley and Horsham in the south east, and South Yorkshire.

The three-year project sets out to identify the range of accommodation provision available and to set this out in a housing directory published annually; and to establish a Multi-Agency Monitoring (MAM) system which can help to establish trends in youth homelessness by reporting twice a year on the records collected. The MAM and Directory information will be drawn together along with more detailed data gathered in qualitative interviews in final reports at the end of the three years. Below is set out some of the information reported in the six-monthly MAM reports published at the end of 1997. This reports on the information collected from agencies between November 1996 and October 1997 (Morton 1997; Prime 1997; Stone 1997).

The information from the MAM reports is based on records submitted from the relevant agencies in each area. Although this includes a small number of statutory agencies, the voluntary sector organisations predominate and so, for the purposes of this chapter, the information is valid and useful. The number of participating agencies varies with South Yorkshire being the largest. Taking that area as an example, 27 agencies participated and recorded a total of 2070 individuals aged 15 to 25 years who approached them for help with their housing problems. Of those agencies, two-thirds were voluntary sector accommodation providers, six provided advice and support services and three were statutory agencies.

The role of the voluntary sector

The MAM shows that a significant proportion of young people approaching the participating agencies are under 18 years old. In South Yorkshire and Crawley/Horsham the proportion was 39 per cent and 42 per cent of all young people recorded respectively. In Lincolnshire, the proportion was slightly lower at 29 per cent. These are young people for whom it is extremely difficult to obtain benefits or to secure access to housing in either the private or social housing sectors. In many cases, these young people may be eligible for some help under the 1989 Children Act and the 1996 Housing Act.

The relationship between voluntary and statutory agencies in the delivery of services to young people is crucial. The section above highlighted the need for voluntary agencies to be able to refer young people back to statutory services as well as to receive referrals. This was seen as particularly important in connection with the very young or vulnerable. As one of the researchers points out:

> The voluntary agencies should not, however, overlook the fact that in some cases a statutory duty may be owed to the young person because of vulnerability or need [under the 1996 Housing Act, 1989 Children Act], if in doubt proper assessments should always be requested. (Prime 1997, p.8)

For some young people voluntary sector services are nevertheless thought to be preferable. One of the researchers notes that '…many young people approach the local voluntary agencies before or instead of going to their local authority' (Prime 1997, p.8). Hence the importance of clear service agreements between statutory agencies and those in the voluntary sector facilitating the discharge of statutory duties under the Act.

One of the difficulties identified above with over-reliance on voluntary action to meet the needs of young homeless people, is the historic failure of the sector to achieve a comprehensive range of services. In Crawley/Horsham, for example, the monitoring found that for young people under the age of 18, there is no direct access or emergency accommodation.

The lack of emergency accommodation can severely limit the options open to a young person who needs or feels the need to leave their accommodation suddenly and without preparation. The monitoring shows that the breakdown of family relationships was the largest single contributory factor to homelessness among the young people recorded in each of the three areas. The proportion for whom this was listed as a factor was 47 per cent in Crawley/Horsham and in South Yorkshire, and 22 per cent in Lincolnshire. The researchers found a number of other factors which may be linked to the need to find new accommodation quickly, for example harassment and breakdown of a relationship with a partner.

By far the largest contributory factor to a young person's housing problem was family breakdown, at 47 per cent. Family breakdown was particularly prevalent amongst females at 68 per cent. It is of some concern that 12 per cent of females had also suffered some form of harassment or abuse that had contributed to their housing problem. (Morton 1997, p.21)

It is also necessary for voluntary agencies to have access to statutory services where their users require mainstream housing. Due to the difficulties experienced by young people in obtaining social security benefits including housing benefit, and problems with obtaining social housing without a guarantor, the monitoring highlights the many other barriers faced by young people.

Means of access to the voluntary sector

Overall, the most common method of referral was by the individual getting in touch with an agency directly, or through family or friends. These kinds of referral accounted for around 40 per cent of all referrals recorded in South Yorkshire and Crawley/Horsham, and in Lincolnshire for well over half of all referrals at about 60 per cent. This finding adds emphasis to the importance of making voluntary services easily accessible both practically and administratively. The monitoring suggested that this is particularly important in rural areas. This is linked to the finding in Lincolnshire that for many young people contact with services comes some time after they first become homeless.

> ...it was apparent that many young people in housing need did not seek advice or assistance from local agencies. Instead they relied on friends and families for support. In many cases, they did not make contact with voluntary or statutory agencies until they were some way into their *homelessness careers*. (Stone 1997)

Conclusion

This chapter has examined some of the issues surrounding young homeless people's access to services in the voluntary sector. It has sought to provide some background to the sector, its relationship with statutory services and the ways in which young people obtain services. The second part of the chapter provided supporting evidence drawn from agency monitoring carried out in three geographical areas. Last, in this chapter, it has been suggested that alongside access to voluntary services, there is a need to consider the ability of the voluntary sector to help young people obtain statutory services; and to

---

Box 12.1 Case study A

Polly is a 16-year-old woman who contacted a young single homelessness project. She had become homeless after being physically assaulted by her father during an argument. For the first weekend she had stayed with friends, but she could not stay with them for any longer. Polly was in full-time education and had no income. She was not able to obtain accommodation in the area in which she lived, because the only housing available were very expensive properties for rent privately. Polly was therefore referred to a local emergency accommodation service. She spent two weeks there while the homelessness project negotiated on her behalf with the local social services department. She was then placed in a foster home for one month in order to complete her school examinations. Because of her circumstances she was exempt from usual housing benefit restrictions for young people and was thus able to secure self-contained accommodation in the private rented sector. As a result she was able to continue her education and went on to further studies at the local college.

---

examine how young people can be helped to stay in touch with services or sustain accommodation once access has been obtained.

Recommendations

- There is a need to promote the development of young people's housing strategies, in order to prevent and alleviate homelessness through the provision of a comprehensive network of housing and support services.

- There is a need to promote the co-ordination of voluntary action with statutory services to ensure a coherent service to young people with agreed standards of provision.

- There is a need to maintain access to statutory services for young people who require social housing or social services support or for whom voluntary provision is unsuitable.

Box 12.2 Case study B

Martin was 16 years old when he contacted a service for young people. He had become homeless after his relationship with his parents had broken down. Little is known of his background, but in the past he had been assessed as having special educational needs. Martin lived in an area where he could not afford the kind of accommodation available. Initially, he went to stay in local emergency accommodation, later moving to a hostel some 20 miles away. The hostel placement broke down after three days due to friction between Martin and other residents. The local social services department was asked to help find an alternative, but this too proved unsuccessful. A privately rented bed-sit was found for Martin and he was offered extra support from the social services department. However, he lost this accommodation after it was discovered that he was setting fire to things in his room. He was unable to return to emergency accommodation, because of his record of playing with fire. Instead, social services funded a short-term bed and breakfast placement while an alternative was sought. That alternative was another voluntary sector project offering a medium level of support and located 35 miles from his home town. This placement also broke down after female staff complained about Martin's behaviour towards them. Martin is now living in private rented accommodation and is not receiving any support. The social services authority agrees that he needs a placement that will offer him a safe environment and intensive support. If he was 18 years old, this would be possible. However, there are no facilities of this kind for 16 year olds in the county, and suitable placements outside the county are prohibitively expensive.

Acknowledgement

The Multi-Agency Monitoring of young people in housing need is part of the Shelter Network Project supported by Midland Bank.

CHAPTER 13

Family Homelessness in the USA

John C. Buckner and Ellen L. Bassuk

Overview of homelessness in the USA

The shelter 'system' in the USA has evolved in the past two decades to meet the needs of growing numbers of homeless persons comprising three distinct sub-groups: single adults; unaccompanied homeless adolescents (i.e. run-away and homeless youths); and the subject of this chapter, homeless families with children. In the following pages, we review the problem of family homelessness in the USA by discussing findings from studies conducted in multiple cities, focusing particularly on a longitudinal study of homeless and low income housed families which we and our colleagues have been conducting in Massachusetts.

Homelessness has been an endemic problem in the USA throughout much of its history, but did not become a crisis until the last 20 years. Visitors to America in the 1950s and 1960s might have noticed only a few individuals and virtually no families on our city streets. The 'literally homeless', that is those lacking a fixed, regular, and adequate night-time residence, were primarily middle-aged men living on the margins of society with few ties to relatives (Caton 1990; Rossi 1989). Residing predominantly in inexpensive hotels within the 'Skid Row' confines of America's inner cities, their housing status was characterised more by the lack of a 'home' – a place of habitation shared with loved ones – than by the literal absence of shelter. These men typically had alcohol problems, were isolated from the rest of society, and had difficulties finding and keeping employment during periods of strong economic growth and prosperity.

Due to a confluence of economic, social policy, and demographic factors in the mid-1980s, American homelessness was transformed: the absolute numbers of homeless persons skyrocketed, the composition of the homeless population changed, and the visibility of the problem increased. Part of the reason for the dramatic increase in the number of homeless persons during this period can be attributed to the baby boom: 76.5 million Americans were born between 1947 to 1964, representing a dramatic population increase. Due to sheer numbers, this cohort of individuals has significantly taxed this nation's institutions and resources, including its housing stock.

In addition to these demographic factors, changes in mental health policy had a pronounced impact on the composition of the homeless population (Bassuk 1984). With the introduction of the phenothiazines to treat the symptoms of severe mental illness, numerous individuals who previously needed to be hospitalised could reside in the community and many psychiatric hospitals were closed. The expectation was that community-based mental health centres would stabilise and support these patients outside the hospital. However, alternatives, especially supported housing linked to comprehensive outpatient mental health services, were not available in many areas.

As a result of the faulty implementation of deinstitutionalisation, increasing numbers of men and women with schizophrenia and other forms of severe mental illness joined the ranks of the homeless (Bassuk 1984; Fischer and Breakey 1991). In addition, as the gentrification of American cities progressed, inexpensive single room occupancy (SRO) hotels – which had provided modest accommodations to some individuals with serious alcohol or mental health problems – were being converted into condominiums. Razing of SRO housing without suitable replacement catapulted many single adults onto the streets and made their plight much more visible.

Macrolevel causes of family homelessness

For first time since the Great Depression, family homelessness became a significant issue in the USA, beginning in the 1980s. The genesis of family homelessness in America involves income, employment, housing, and demographic factors (Rossi 1994). The disparity between the incomes of the rich and poor slowly increased in the 1970s and grew more rapidly during the early 1980s (US Bureau of the Census 1996). From 1968 to 1994, average household incomes among the wealthiest 20 per cent of households increased by 44 per cent from $73,754 to $105,945, whereas incomes in the bottom quintile increased only eight per cent from $7202 to $7762. In the past 25 years, improvements in technology as well as job competition from third world countries have led to reduced wages and increased unemployment for those with limited education and employment skills. The availability of fewer jobs paying a decent wage has particularly affected the living standards of young adults and minority group members, many of whom spend an inordinate percentage of their income on housing, thereby increasing the pool of individuals and families at risk for homelessness.

Up until 1996, Aid to Families with Dependent Children (AFDC) was the major federal programme providing cash assistance to families in need. However, the absolute dollar amount of cash assistance to poor families has largely remained constant since the mid-1970s. Hence, due to inflation, the purchasing power of a monthly AFDC cheque has steadily eroded, making it increasingly difficult for families to pay for food, rent, and other essentials.

Another major factor contributing to the growth of family homelessness has been the failure of public and private entities to build or rehabilitate enough low income housing units to keep pace with the growing number of families. In 1970, affordable housing was plentiful in America but by 1989 a substantial gap had emerged between the supply (2.8 million residences) and demand (7.8 million renter households) for housing among households in the bottom income quartile (Koegel, Burnam and Baumohl 1996).

Finally, the last several decades have seen a steady increase in the number of single parent (mostly female-headed) families in America. The bleak economic prospects of many inner-city men along with restrictions in welfare benefits for two-parent families are two important reasons why fewer two-parent families have been forming, especially among the poor in the USA (Ellwood 1988; Jencks 1992; Wilson 1987). Single parent families are usually poorer than two-parent families due, in part, to the presence of a single income and the cost of child care. The increase in the number of single parent families, many of whom lack sufficient economic and social resources, is another important contributing cause of family homelessness in this country.

In summary, a constellation of factors explains the rise in family homelessness in America during the last two decades. These factors help explain why homelessness has become a major social problem but do not shed light on who is most likely to experience this condition. In the next section, we briefly discuss the family shelter system in this country and then review research findings describing the characteristics of homeless families in America as well as risk factors for becoming homeless.

The US family shelter system

An extensive array of family shelters, loosely forming a system, has arisen in the past two decades to respond to emergency requests for temporary housing (Weinreb and Buckner 1993; Weinreb and Rossi 1995). Reflecting a rise in the incidence and duration of family homelessness, the US Department of Housing and Urban Development (1989) estimated that, among cities of 25,000 or more, the number of shelters increased from about 1900 in 1984 to more than 5000 in 1988. More recent reliable estimates of the number of family shelters in the USA, their average nightly census, and the number of families homeless in a year are not available.

Due to this sizable shelter infrastructure that exists across the USA, the experience of homelessness for families almost always takes the form of a shelter stay that can last for several days for some, several months for most, and a year or more for a few. While some families live in cars or camp indefinitely in public parks, particularly during the summer or in regions of the country where the winter climate is mild, they are exceptions. Unlike homelessness among single adults, family homelessness in America is virtually synonymous with living in shelter.

Family shelters are generally of three types: a) emergency shelters that provide housing and some social services to parent(s) and children for usually less than four months; b) transitional shelters that provide longer-term housing and services; and c) shelters for women fleeing abusive relationships (i.e. battered women's shelters). The majority of shelters are privately funded as their primary source of financial support although some shelters receive significant funding from local, state, and federal sources as well. Either directly or indirectly (through referrals to other community agencies), most family shelters provide food/meals, case management, assistance securing entitlements/benefits and housing, substance abuse counselling, parenting education, transportation, child care, medical care, nutritional education, and early intervention services for children (Weinreb and Rossi 1995).

Characteristics of homeless families

According to a recent annual 29-city survey conducted by the US Conference of Mayors (1996), the composition of the overall homeless population includes: (45%) single men, (14%) single women, (38%) families with children, and (3%) unaccompanied adolescents. Children represent 27 per cent of all homeless individuals.

The structure of homeless families varies depending upon geographic region. In the Northeast, in cities such as New York and Boston, homeless families are almost all single-parent female-headed (i.e. 95%). In the South and Southwest, in states such as Florida and Arizona, approximately 30 per cent are two-parent families. Families who become homeless emerge from the broader population of poor families within a community; hence, they tend to mirror the larger group in terms of sociodemographic characteristics. In places such as Baltimore and Washington D.C., they are almost exclusively African-American.

In Worcester, Massachusetts (a mid-sized city 30 miles due west of Boston) where we and our colleagues have been conducting a comprehensive longitudinal study of homeless and low-income (never homeless) mothers and children since 1992 (see Bassuk *et al.* 1996 and 1997a), the majority of homeless mothers are either white of Northern European descent (33%) or are Hispanic (43%), mostly of Puerto Rican heritage. In spite of regional variation, African Americans are greatly over-represented (roughly 60%) among both homeless single adults and homeless families in comparison to the proportion in the general US population (12.5%).

According to a study of homeless families in nine major American cities, the typical homeless family is comprised of a single mother, 30 years of age, with two children under five years (Rog *et al.* 1995). About half of the mothers have never married. Most families have incomes significantly below the poverty line of $12,156 for a family of three in 1995. For example, in Worcester, homeless families had an average income of $7910. In Rog and coworkers' nine city study, 58 per cent of mothers had obtained a high school degree or its equivalent, comparable to the rate of 54 per cent in Worcester. Two-thirds of mothers in our study have had prior work experience, but only one per cent were currently employed.

Homeless families tend to live in unstable situations prior to becoming homeless. In Worcester, families had moved 3.8 times on average in the two years prior to entering shelter and only 18 per cent were primary tenants (i.e. held a lease in their name) immediately before becoming homeless. Their median shelter stay was approximately eight weeks with a range of 1–51 weeks. While the length of shelter stay varies across the nation, in general, homelessness is a temporary and sometimes episodic state for families (and individuals) as opposed to an enduring experience (Shinn 1997).

Factors influencing vulnerability to family homelessness

Researchers in America have likened homelessness to the game of *musical chairs*, an activity premised on creating a situation in which more people are present than there are chairs in which they can sit (Buckner, Bassuk, and Zima 1993; Koegel *et al.* 1996; Sclar 1990). The analogy illustrates two levels of analysis: the macro or structural-level (e.g. an imbalance between supply and demand), which is the root cause and the individual-level (e.g. characteristics and attributes of individuals) where causal attributions can mistakenly be made.

For example, in this game, the issue of why people are left standing when the music stops has to do with the structural imbalance between the number of chairs and people, and nothing to do with the traits or qualities of the individual participants. On the other hand, who is most vulnerable to losing the competitive struggle, whether it be for a chair or affordable housing, relates to risk and protective factors regarding one's ability to compete successfully. For instance, substance use problems, mental illness, and caring for dependent children are attributes that are over-represented among homeless persons. Yet, they should be regarded as important factors (among others) which, at the individual-level, help explain differences in vulnerability to homelessness rather than answer why homelessness exists as an international social problem.

Using univariate statistics, researchers in New York City (Shinn, Knickman, and Weitzman 1991; Weitzman, Knickman, and Shin 1992), Los Angeles (Wood *et al.* 1990), and Boston (Bassuk and Rosenberg 1988; Goodman 1991a and 1991b) have examined mental health, violence, and social support-related variables that may increase vulnerability to family homelessness. Results have been inconsistent across each of these domains. Discrepancies may be due to differences in the timing of assessments, the type of comparison group selected, and the contextual circumstances within the city in which a particular study was conducted.

Recently, we reported our results of risk and protective factors for family homelessness in Worcester (Bassuk *et al.* 1997a). This study employed multivariate analyses to examine both the independent and relative contribution of potential variables that could account for the differential vulnerability of families to homelessness. This study compared 220 mothers living in Worcester's nine family shelters to 216 low income housed mothers who had never been homeless.

Since family homelessness in our region of the country is almost exclusively experienced by single mothers with children in tow, we did not enroll any two-parent families. A methodological challenge we faced was finding a comparison group of families who had never experienced homelessness, but who were at economic risk. Hence, we enrolled the comparison group by approaching women who were coming to Worcester's Department of Public Welfare to see their caseworker regarding their continued eligibility to receive AFDC.

Mothers in both the homeless and housed groups received similar interviews. In addition to asking about demographics, we asked detailed questions about housing and employment, income and receipt of benefits, social support, and resources of individuals in their social network, and conducted clinical interviews of their mental health status, which include lifetime and current diagnoses of psychiatric and substance use disorders. We also carefully assessed experiences of victimisation, including childhood physical and sexual abuse and recent violence from an adult male partner as well as questions pertaining to other potentially traumatic events such as foster care placement during childhood.

Based on previous research conducted in the mid-1980s (see Bassuk 1991; Bassuk and Rosenberg 1988), we had expected that homeless compared to housed mothers would have more mental health and substance use problems, be more likely to have been physically and/or sexually assaulted, and have smaller social networks with fewer tangible resources among network members. To our surprise, these expectations (with the exception of social support) were not confirmed by our results (see Bassuk *et al.* 1996 and 1997a). While we found economic differences between homeless and housed mothers that could account for their housing status, there were remarkable similarities in terms of histories of violent victimisation as well as mental health and substance use problems.

Among the women in our study, an appalling 92 per cent of the homeless and 82 per cent of the housed mothers experienced severe physical and/or sexual assaults at some point in their lives as measured by the Conflict Tactics Scales. More than 40 per cent in both groups were sexually abused as children. Similarly, high rates of violent victimisation have also been documented by Rog *et al.* (1995) in their nine city study. Using the same measure, they found that 65 per cent of the 743 women in their study reported one or more severe acts of violence by a current or former intimate partner. Goodman (1991a) also found comparably high rates of domestic violence in her studies of poor and homeless families in Massachusetts. A recent statewide survey of mothers receiving welfare in Massachusetts indicated that one-third were currently in violent relationships (Allard *et al.* 1997).

Likewise, rates and patterns of lifetime and current mental disorders were comparable for both homeless and housed mothers. These disorders may have resulted from the combined effects of unremitting stressors including pervasive violence. More than 40 per cent of both groups were in a major depression (twice the rate of the general female population), more than one-third had experienced post traumatic stress disorder (three time the rate of the general female population), and 38 per cent had experienced a substance use problem during their lifetimes.

In addition, over one-third of both groups had a clinical diagnosis within the previous 30 days, with the same three disorders having elevated prevalence. Thirty-one per cent of homeless mothers and 26 per cent of housed mothers had attempted suicide at least once, usually in adolescence. Compared with the general population of women aged 25 to 34 years, both homeless and housed mothers had poorer physical health and more chronic health conditions (Weinreb, Goldberg, and Perloff, in press).

Many of the women in the Worcester study were extremely isolated and had few personal, institutional, or community supports. Homeless mothers had fewer non-professional network members compared to the housed, but both groups had extremely small networks (4.0 people in their network *vs.* 4.6). In addition to fewer social ties, the homeless had more conflicted relationships and were less willing to seek support than the housed mothers. Furthermore, the network members of the homeless had fewer basic resources such as money, food, and housing.

In terms of factors which could account for the different housing status of the two groups, multivariate modelling demonstrated that factors protective against family homelessness include a housing subsidy, AFDC, graduating from high school, having more people in one's social network, and having fewer conflicted relationships (Bassuk *et al.* 1997a). In addition, factors that reduce an individual's economic and/or social capital were associated with homelessness. For example, mental hospitalisation within the last two years and frequent use of alcohol or heroin were risk factors.

Although we had hypothesised that violent victimisation might severely compromise a mother's resources, due to its pervasiveness in both groups it did not emerge as a risk factor for family homelessness. Housing subsidies were a particularly important protective factor in our analyses due to the strength of their association with housing status and the proportion of families in the comparison group who received this benefit (27%). In contrast, such factors as use of heroin and mental hospitalisation were strongly associated with homelessness but were uncommon behaviours or events (e.g. only 5% of homeless and 1% of housed mothers had used heroin in the past two years) and therefore could not explain vulnerability to homelessness for the vast majority of homeless families.

While the Worcester study has many strengths, including the comprehensive nature of the assessments, a carefully selected comparison group, large sample size, and multivariate analyses of the data, it is obviously limited to one mid-sized American city. However, with the exception of the high proportion of Latinos and modest representation of African Americans, our study participants are representative of other homeless and low income families in the USA (see Bassuk *et al.* 1997a for further details). Our findings suggest that psychosocial variables are subordinate to more tangible economic variables in explaining mothers' differential vulnerability to family homelessness. The data also point to the tremendous need for violence prevention programs and policies as well as mental health treatment in order to improve the lives of extremely poor women.

Homeless children

Research conducted on homeless children in America during the 1980s and early 1990s reported a high absolute prevalence of rates of health problems (Alperstein, Rappaport and Flanigan 1988; Parker *et al.* 1991; Rafferty and Shinn 1991), developmental delays (Bassuk and Rosenberg 1990; Miller and Lin 1988; Molnar and Rath 1990; Wood *et al.* 1990), and emotional and behavioural difficulties (Bassuk and Rosenberg 1990; Molnar and Rath 1990; Wood *et al.* 1990; Zima, Wells and Freeman 1994). When comparison groups comprised of children of similar age who were living in housing were also assessed, homeless children usually looked worse on measures of developmental status, behaviour problems, school performance and health (see Bassuk and Rosenburg 1990; Molnar *et al.* 1991).

However, even including studies with a comparison group, this first generation of research did not examine whether differences between homeless and housed children were attributable to housing status *per se*, or to other explanatory variables, such as mother's mental health status or drug use. These potentially 'confounding' factors could account for both the current housing status of the family as well as differences between homeless and housed children on outcome measures.

A second generation of research began in the early 1990s to address the methodological limitations of this earlier research. Some of these studies (including our own in Worcester) were funded by the National Institute of Mental Health within the US Department of Health and Human Services. Surprisingly, these projects have not reported the same magnitude of differences between homeless and housed children described in previous studies. For example, in a study of 159 homeless and 62 low-income housed children conducted in Minneapolis, Masten and colleagues (1993) found that mothers' psychological distress, exposure to negative life events, and a summary count of various risk indicators were predictive of behaviour problems, whereas housing status was not.

Likewise, Rubin and coworkers (1996) examined the relation between housing status and cognitive abilities and academic achievement among 102 homeless and 178 housed school-age children in New York City. Controlling for demographic characteristics, verbal and nonverbal measures of intelligence were not different between the two groups of children, but homeless children scored lower on a measure of academic achievement.

In the Worcester study, we have found more pronounced differences between homeless and housed school-age children than among the younger children but not on all variables. For example, Buckner and colleagues (in press) found that homeless children evidenced greater internalising problem behaviours (withdrawn, anxious, depressive behaviours) as reported by mothers compared to their housed counterparts even when controlling for a multitude of other explanatory variables. However, differences were not found on externalising problem behaviours or on child self-reported measures of depression and anxiety.

Similarly, we examined children of nine years and older to find out whether they met criteria for a range of psychiatric diagnoses and found that homeless and low-income housed children had comparable current prevalence rates (e.g. approximately 32% of youths in both groups had at least one current psychiatric disorder, Buckner and Bassuk 1997). At the same time, these rates were significantly above the comparable prevalence rate of 19 per cent found for youths in the general population (Shaffer *et al.* 1996).

These commonalities extended to younger children as well. Using the Bayley Scales of Infant Development, a state-of-the-art measure of developmental status, we documented that homeless and housed infants and toddlers scored almost identically (Garcia-Coll *et al.* in press). In addition, housing status was not a significant predictor of problem behaviour among pre-school age children (Bassuk *et al.* 1997b). Rather, mothers' psychological distress was the most salient explanatory variable. In short, the findings of recent research highlight similarities between the life events and adjustment of homeless and poor (never homeless) children as opposed to stark differences.

These results seem to suggest that while homelessness is a stressful experience for most children, it is unfortunately just one of a number of acute events and chronic stressors affecting children living in poverty. Other events and strains, such as experiences of physical and sexual abuse, witnessing violence, out-of-home placement, hunger, and parental mental health and substance use problems also explain differences in the mental health and behaviour of these children.

Mary, a sweet and engaging nine-year-old girl of northern European descent, typifies the circumstances of many homeless children in our study. Mary, along with her mother, Joan, and her eleven-year-old brother, Robert, became homeless after they were evicted from their run-down apartment in a crime-ridden public housing project. Joan, who had a history of alcohol and drug abuse and drug-related arrests as well as symptoms of post-traumatic stress disorder, went to a shelter that helped women overcome their drug addictions.

The family had been living there for four months prior to participating in our study. Mary described symptoms of anxiety and depression when we interviewed her in the shelter. She was mainly concerned about her mother's drug problem and its effects on her life. Mary had been placed in foster homes on two separate occasions and had been physically abused by a foster parent. In the past year, in addition to losing her home and coping with her mother's drug use, Mary had been in a foster home for a month, had gone to three different schools, had experienced her mother's arrest for shoplifting, and had observed several violent encounters between her parents leading up to their divorce. In addition to these events, Mary also reported that she did not get enough to eat, felt unsafe because of the crime in her neighbourhood, and was concerned about the well-being of her father, brother, and mother.

When we asked Mary about her shelter stay during a follow-up interview two years later, her reactions were mixed. Despite finding the shelter to have various annoying restrictions, Mary also said she made friends with some other children her age who were also living there. She had also received both individual and group counselling from shelter staff members, which she found helpful. In short, Mary is a child who has been besieged by a number of acute negative events and chronic strains in her life, of which her shelter stay was one of many. Her story is by no means unusual and exemplifies a broad set of issues, in addition to homelessness, that children living in poverty in America must confront.

Recommendations

Given the political will, much can be done to prevent family homelessness. Preventive strategies include building more affordable housing for low income families, financing additional rental subsidies/vouchers, and making it easier for families on the verge of eviction to obtain emergency rental assistance.

The incidence of homelessness can also be reduced by addressing other needs of low income individuals and families. These include providing training and enough jobs that pay livable wages, accessible health care for all, safe and affordable child care, and public transportation to get to and from work. In addition, enforcement of child support payments and government-sponsored child support assurance (a base monthly child support payment to the custodial parent when the non-custodial parent is unable or unwilling to pay) would greatly help low-income single-parent families without creating disincentives to work (Garfinkel 1992 and 1994).

Just as homelessness is linked to poverty, both are affected by broader societal issues such as the state of a nation's schools and its economy. The educational system is critical in preparing young people for the work force, as is job training for adults with limited skills. Economic and social policies which help to create more jobs that foster self-sufficiency are essential for alleviating poverty and homelessness.

For those currently in shelter, family-based case management is important in order to help families find housing and tangible assistance that will help them become more residentially stable. Parent(s) and children should be worked with simultaneously as a family. While the specific treatment and educational needs of children should be addressed in a developmentally appropriate fashion, helping parent(s) is also critical for ensuring the long-term benefit of the child. For example, our research highlights pervasive histories of violent victimisation of the mothers and indicates the need for appropriate treatment whether in shelter or in the community (Bassuk, Melnick and Browne 1998).

Conclusion

Family homelessness first emerged as a pressing social problem for the USA in the mid-1980s and has steadily grown in the past 15 years. Family shelters have sprung up in communities across America as a stop-gap measure to house families in crisis. By necessity they have become permanent fixtures and are the lowest rung in the housing market for poor households (Rossi 1994).

Current research findings suggest that the plight of poor families is worsening in this country. This is evidenced by the high absolute rates of stressors and extreme financial deprivation that families must deal with and the increased similarity between homeless and poor housed families in terms of violent victimisation, mental and physical health problems, and other domains.

Recent political events give cause for concern that poverty and increased rates of homelessness among families will only worsen in the USA in the years ahead (Bassuk, Browne and Buckner 1996). In 1996, the US Congress passed landmark legislation to reform the welfare system and abolish AFDC. This legislation transferred power from the federal-level to state and local governments and required states to set time limits on the availability of funds as well as work requirements. The ramifications of this reform are as yet unclear.

In a strong economy, some families will be induced to leave the welfare rolls and find reasonable paid employment. However, jobs that pay enough for a single mother to be self-supporting are few and decent child care is expensive. Hence, many poor families will find it increasingly difficult to make ends meet.

Our study findings and those of others suggest that both homeless and other low income families are in strong need of a range of supports to help them secure stable housing, food, health care, child care, and job training. Turning its back on the desperate reality described above, our nation has embarked on a series of 'get tough' social reforms that will probably create significant added hardships for most poor families. An increase in the incidence and duration of homelessness is one likely negative repercussion, as more and more families previously assisted by AFDC lose this benefit. Despite the considerable power and prestige that the USA enjoys in the world today, care and concern for its least advantaged citizens is not something for which this country can presently be proud.

CHAPTER 14

Responding to Family Homelessness

Stuart Cumella and Panos Vostanis

Key themes

The contributions included in this book are by researchers from different professional backgrounds and different countries. But some key themes emerge consistently:

- The population of homeless families and children is heterogeneous and there is a high turnover of families moving into and out of homelessness, and between different types of temporary accommodation. Official statistics under-estimate the true extent of homelessness among families and children by excluding people who live in temporary accommodation but do not apply to their local authority for rehousing, and people categorised by local authorities as 'intentionally homeless'.

- The majority of families admitted to emergency homeless accommodation are headed by single women, with poor financial or social resources, who have experienced sustained violence from partners, ex-partners, or neighbours. By contrast, a high proportion of single homeless adolescents have been in local authority care, or have experienced sexual or other physical abuse, or parental discord. For both groups, becoming homeless was often a personal solution to intolerable circumstances.

- There are substantial local variations in the availability of emergency homeless accommodation for families, the type of accommodation provided, and the duration of stay before rehousing. Even in well-managed homeless centres, many families experience stress as a result of limited space (particularly play space for children), and a difficulty in maintaining the routines of family life.

- Children in homeless families have greater developmental delay than low income families in stable housing, higher levels of infectious diseases, and higher rates of accidents. This is particularly the case with families in multi-occupied temporary accommodation managed by the private sector.

- There is a high rate of mental health problems among both parents and children in homeless centres. These are often caused by the adverse events which precipitated homelessness, but also by the loss of a stable home and the removal from the protection provided by school and friendships. Mental health problems are most common among children whose mothers themselves have psychiatric disorders, and who are socially isolated. There is evidence that mental health problems persist among children even after resettlement in stable housing.

- Families in homeless centres in England have high levels of contact with primary health care, although the effectiveness of these contacts may be limited by problems in accessing medical records for patients on a temporary registration. In common with other low income families in urban areas, homeless families also have high rates of contact with hospital outpatient departments. Contacts with social workers are also higher than among other low income families, probably because of child protection issues. Few homeless families and very few children receive help from specialist mental health services.

- Parents in homeless families demonstrate an ability to generate their own solutions to problems, and retain the hope of returning to stable housing and re-entering the labour market. Access to affordable social housing plays a crucial part in enabling families to achieve these goals. In its absence, a substantial number of homeless families move between a series of short-term placements in poor quality temporary housing. This outcome is particularly disruptive for family life and for children's education, and poses a higher risk for both parents and children of disease, accidents, social isolation, and mental health problems.

The contributors to this book have also identified some areas in which knowledge is currently limited, and where further investigation is required. These include:

- Research and development into methods for preventing homelessness among families. This should include an evaluation of the impact of the housing advice available to people facing homelessness required by the 1996 Housing Act, and the extent to which concerted action by the criminal justice system, housing authorities, and social services departments can prevent people becoming homeless to avoid domestic or neighbourhood violence.

- An evaluative review of local initiatives for ensuring access for homeless families to health and social care, and for supporting homeless families in parenting. These should pay particular attention to schemes which designate specialist teams or staff to work with homeless families.

- An evaluation of the impact of providing enhanced training for staff in homeless centres and in other facilities which admit homeless families and their children.

- Measurement of the long-term impact of homelessness on the development and mental and physical health of children, including both families who are resettled into stable housing, and those which become long-term residents in temporary housing.

A strategy for family homelessness

This book has confirmed that homeless families and single homeless adolescents have multiple problems, which require a sustained and co-ordinated response from housing authorities, schools, social services, independent providers of welfare services, the criminal justice system, and primary and specialist health services. This should have the aims of:

- Preventing homelessness by protecting families from violence and intimidation from partners, ex-partners, and neighbours.

- Ensuring access to a high quality of emergency accommodation which does not place families at additional risk of accidents or ill health.

- Maintaining continuity of school attendance for children in homeless families.

- Ensuring access for homeless families to appropriate health and social care.
- Providing rapid access to affordable and permanent housing, to minimise the risk of personal and family breakdown.

The attainment of these objectives requires:

- Local multi-agency forums to identify the numbers and needs of homeless families and adolescents, to develop and monitor a strategy for family homelessness, and to act as advocates for more effective local policies.
- The designation of homeless children and families as a group whose needs should be routinely reviewed in policy documents and annual reports produced by local housing, health, education, and social services.
- The designation of senior managers in local education authorities, social services departments, and health authorities, who have responsibility for agency policy towards homeless families.
- Greater sharing of information about homelessness between local agencies, to allow early detection and assessment of high risk families (particularly regarding child protection issues) and knowledge of disabilities and special needs. There should also be improvements in the transmission of personal medical records between primary care teams.

Action by central and local government to prevent homelessness requires:

- Central government to review current legislation, to identify changes which would ensure greater protection for families who are victims of violence from partners, ex-partners, or neighbours.
- Local authorities to ensure rapid access for families facing homelessness to advice and assistance, including advice on re-assigning tenancies and legal advice on protection from violence.

Action to ensure access to emergency housing for homeless families requires:

- Local housing authorities to phase out the use of poor quality temporary housing, and aim to provide access for homeless families to centres which meet health and safety standards, provide acceptable facilities for families (including indoor and outdoor play areas for the children), and which have trained staff.

- Central government to require local housing authorities to conform to specified definitions of homelessness and intentionality. Central monitoring should record the numbers of homeless families who apply for rehousing, the number and ages of children, the outcome of applications (both in terms of placement in temporary accommodation and resettlement in permanent housing), and time-lag between application and resettlement.

Continuity of schooling for children in homeless families requires the following action:

- Local education authorities to monitor the distribution of homeless children, and take this into account in the allocation of funding to primary and secondary schools. This should take account of the additional expenditure incurred in transport, school uniforms and school meals.

- Schools used by families in homeless centres need to have spare capacity to meet fluctuating demand, and should provide flexible learning opportunities and teaching methods for homeless pupils. Befriending schemes and other measures should be developed to increase homeless pupils' re-integration into schools in cases where there have been long absences.

Ensuring access to healthcare and social services for homeless families requires:

- Each homeless centre or facility to be the focus of a local network of health, education, and social services. The primary healthcare teams used by each centre should have designated sessions for health visitors to work with homeless families, organise multi-skill assessments, and be responsible for ensuring that families and children are appropriately referred to local services following rehousing.

- Health and social services to commission designated sessions for paediatrists, psychiatrists, educational psychologists, community nurses, social workers, and health visitors, to work with homeless families.

- Training to be provided for staff in homeless centres, to help them identify mental health problems and refer appropriately. Training should also be available for keyworkers or client advocates, to enable them to provide counselling for clients rather than just mediating between existing (and usually under-resourced) mainstream services.

- Immediate access for families in homeless facilities to local nurseries, child minding services, and drop-in centres.

Some additional steps are required to meet the needs of single homeless adolescents:

- An increased input of counselling for young people in the care system, as well as an improved aftercare service. These should aim to promote life skills and problem-solving skills, improve educational and employment opportunities, and (where appropriate) to sustain contact with families and social networks.

- The provision of outreach health care to single adolescents, and an improved mental health service for adolescents, particularly for depression, self-harm, substance misuse and impulse control problems.

Last, it should be emphasised that the keystone of services for homeless families should be rapid resettlement in affordable and permanent housing. This requires a policy commitment by central government to attain this objective, coupled with the specification of standards to be achieved by local housing authorities and mechanisms for enforcement. The aim of rehousing should not be merely to provide accommodation, but to ensure the development of a stable and secure home where families can re-establish their lives and provide a nurturing environment for their children.

List of Contributors

Leila Baker is Research Manager at Shelter where she has worked since 1995. Prior to that, she worked as part of the housing and community research team at Southampton University. She has been working in the field of homelessness in a variety of roles for the past ten years.

Jacqueline Barnes, PhD (formerly McGuire) is Senior Lecturer in Psychology at the Leopold Muller Department of Child and Family Mental Health of the Royal Free and University College Medical School and Honorary Senior Psychologist at the Tavistock Clinic, London. Her research interests include the identification, development and management of emotional and behavioural problems in young children, and the relevance of environmental influences such as community characteristics to child development.

Ellen L. Bassuk, M.D, is an Associate Professor of Psychiatry at the Harvard Medical School and President of the Better Homes Fund, Newton, MA, which she co-founded in 1988 to address the needs of homeless families in America. Dr Bassuk conducted the first systematic studies of homeless families in the United States in the mid 1980s. She is the principal researcher of the Worcester Family Research Project.

Caroline Blair is a consultant clinical psychologist at the Young People's Unit, Royal Edinburgh Hospital, and honorary fellow at the University of Edinburgh. Her current research interests concern the recognition and treatment of depression in young people in the community.

John C. Buckner, PhD, a clinical community psychologist, is an instructor in psychiatry at Children's Hospital, Harvard Medical School, and Director of Research at the Better Homes Fund, Newton, MA. Dr Buckner worked from 1989–1991 in the office of Programmes for the Homeless Mentally Ill, US Department of Health and Human Services. He is currently conducting an NIMH-funded study on stress, coping and resilience among children living in poverty.

Stuart Cumella, PhD is Senior Research Fellow at the University of Birmingham Medical School. His first degree was a BSc (Econ) at the London School of Economics; he subsequently obtained an MSc in Politics at the University of

Strathclyde and a Diploma in Social Work at the University of Stirling, before his PhD at the University of London. He has worked as a social worker, a civil service and Medical Research Council researcher, and as a director of planning and information in the NHS. Dr Cumella has carried out many evaluations of community care services, including those for people with a mental illness and homeless families.

Gill Hague is a research fellow and founder member of the Domestic Violence Research Group at the University of Bristol, which conducts national and international studies of domestic violence and wide-ranging consultancy, teaching and training. Together with Ellen Malos, she has carried out a range of studies, for example on housing and domestic violence, and on inter-agency approaches. They have produced many publications on domestic violence including *Domestic Violence: Action for Change* (1998). Gill Hague is an activist of long-standing in the movement against domestic violence.

Kathleen Hutchinson MA RGN RHU CPT is a specialist health visitor for homeless families for the West Berkshire Priority Care Service NHS Trust, and Community Practice Lecturer at the Department of Community Studies at the University of Reading. She is actively involved in collaboration with other agencies to facilitate access to health care for homeless people.

Ellen Malos is a lecturer and a founder member of the Domestic Violence Research Group at the University of Bristol. She has been an activist and a researcher in women's studies, socio-legal studies and domestic violence for many years. Apart from work with Gill Hague, her publications include *The Politics of Housework* (1980 and 1995), *Caring for Other People's Children* (1991) and *You've Got No Life* (1993).

Pat Niner is Senior Lecturer in Housing Studies at the Centre for Urban and Regional Studies, University of Birmingham. She has been involved in a wide variety of housing research studies over more than twenty years, including several projects on homelessness and housing allocations.

Sally Power is Senior Lecturer in Education Policy at the Institute of Education, University of London. Her research interests include all aspects of the sociology of education policy, in particular recent reforms, the relationship between public and private education and the changing nature of the curriculum.

Christina Victor is Reader in Health Service Research at St George's Medical School, Tooting. She has published widely in the field of homelessness and health.

Panos Vostanis is Professor of Child and Adolescent Psychiatry at the University of Leicester. He has developed mental health services for homeless children and young people in care. He has completed research on homeless children and families together with Stuart Cumella.

Geoff Whitty is the Karl Mannheim Professor in the Sociology of Education and Dean of Research at the Institute of Education, University of London. He is interested in education policy and the sociology of education and has conducted research into public and private education, health and welfare, curriculum innovation and teacher education.

Robert Wrate is a consultant in adolescent psychiatry and Honorary Senior Lecturer at the Department of Psychiatry at Royal Edinburgh Hospital. He has published research into patient treamtent of adolescent eating disorders. He is part of the Mental Health NHS workforce, with clinical interests in health equalities, early onset of the psychoses, and family therapy.

Deborah Youdell is a Research Officer in Policy Studies at the Institute of Education, University of London. Her research is broadly concerned with issues of social justice in education. Her recent research has included work on homelessness and education, ethnicity and exclusion from school, and inequalities of experience and outcome in key stage 4 and GCSE examinations.

References

Abrahams, C. and Munsall, R. (1992) *Runaways: Exploding the Myths.* London: National Children's Home.

Achenbach, T. (1992) *Manual for the Child Behaviour Checklist 2 3 and 1992 Profile.* Burlington: University of Vermont Department of Psychiatry.

Achenbach, T. (1991) *Manual for the Child Behaviour Checklist 4 18 and 1991 Profile.* Burlington: University of Vermont Department of Psychiatry.

ACOP (Association of Chief Officers of Probation) (1996) *Position Paper on Domestic Violence.* London: ACOP.

Adams, C., Pantelis, C., Duke, P. and Barnes, T. (1996) 'Psychopathology, social and cognitive functioning in a hostel for homeless women.' *British Journal of Psychiatry 168,* 82–86.

Allard, M.A., Albelda, R., Colten, M.E. and Cosenza, C. (1997) *In Harm's Way?: Domestic Violence, AFDC Receipt, and Welfare Reform in Massachusetts.* Boston: University of Massachusetts.

Alperstein, G., Rappaport, C. and Flanigan, J. (1988) 'Health problems of homeless children in New York City.' *American Journal of Public Health 78,* 1232–1233.

Amery, J., Tomkins, A. and Victor, C.R. (1995) 'The prevalence of behavioural problems amongst homeless primary school children in an outer London borough: a feasibility survey.' *Public Health 109,* 421–424.

Anderson, E.S. (1997) 'Health concerns and needs of traveller families.' *Health Visitor 70,* 148–150.

Angold, A. and Worthman, C.W. (1993) 'Puberty onset of gender differences in depression: a developmental, epidemiologic and neuroendocrine perspective.' *Journal of Affective Disorders 29,* 145–58.

Arden, A. and Hunter, C. (1997) *Homelessness and Allocations: A Guide to the Housing Act 1996.* London: Legal Action Group.

Arden, A. and Hunter, C. (1996) *The Housing Act 1996.* London: Sweet & Maxwell.

Audit Commission (1989) *Housing the Homeless: The Local Authority Role.* London: HMSO.

Avramov, D. (1995) *Homelessness in the European Union: Social and Legal Context of Housing Exclusion in the 1990s.* Brussells: FEANTSA.

Bachrach, L.L. (1992) 'What we know about homelessness among mentally ill persons: an analytical review and commentary.' *Hospital and Community Psychiatry 43,* 453–464.

Bacon, N. (1998) 'Prepared for impact.' *Roof 23,* 34–36.

Baker, L. (1997) *Homelessness and Suicide.* London: Shelter.

Ball, M. (1994) *Funding Refuge Services: a Study of Refuge Support Services for Women and Children Experiencing Domestic Violence.* Bristol: WAFE.

Barnes, J. (1997) 'Methods of measuring community characteristics.' *Child Psychology and Psychiatry Review 2,* 163–169.

Barnes-McGuire, J. (1997) 'The reliability and validity of a questionnaire describing neighbourhood characteristics relevant to families and young children.' *Journal of Community Psychology 25,* 551–566.

Barron, J. (1990) *Not Worth the Paper: The Effectiveness of Legal Protection for Women and Children Experiencing Domestic Violence.* Bristol: WAFE.

Bartlett, S.N. (1997) 'Housing as a factor in the socialization of children: a critical review of the literature.' *Merrill-Palmer Quarterly 43,* 169–198.

Bassuk, E.L. (1984) 'The homeless problem.' *Scientific American 251,* 40–45.

Bassuk, E.L. (1991) 'Homeless families.' *Scientific American 270,* 66–74.

Bassuk, E.L. and Browne, A. (1996) 'The characteristics and needs of sheltered homeless and low-income housed mothers.' *JAMA 276,* 640–646.

Bassuk, E.L., Browne, A. and Buckner, J.C. (1996) 'Single mothers and welfare.' *Scientific American 275,* 60–67.

Bassuk, E., Buckner, J., Weinreb, L., Browne, A., Bassuk, S., Dawson, R. and Perloff, J. (1997) 'Homelessness in female-headed families: childhood and adult risk and protective factors.' *American Journal of Public Health 87,* 241 –248.

Bassuk, E.L., Melnick, S. and Browne, A. (1998) 'Responding to the needs of low-income and homeless women who are survivors of family violence.' *Journal of the American Women's Medical Association 53,* 57–64.

Bassuk, E. and Rosenberg, L. (1988) 'Why does family homelessness occur? A case-control study.' *American Journal of Public Health 78,* 783–788.

Bassuk, E. and Rosenberg, L. (1990) 'Psychosocial characteristics of homeless children and children with homes.'   257–261.

Bassuk, E.L., Rubin, L. and Lauriat, A.S. (1986) 'Characteristics of sheltered homeless families.' *American Journal of Public Health 76,* 1097–1101.

Bassuk, E.L., Weinreb, L.F., Buckner, J.C., Browne, A., Salomon, A. and Bassuk, S.S. (1996) 'The characteristics and needs of sheltered homeless and low-income housed mothers.' *Journal of the American Medical Association 276,* 640–646.

Bassuk, E.L., Weinreb, L.F., Dawson, R., Perloff, J.N. and Buckner, J.C. (1997) 'Determinants of behaviour in sheltered homeless and low-income housed pre-school children.' *Pediatrics 100,* 92–100.

Beardslee, W. (1989) 'The role of self-understanding in resilient individuals: the development of a perspective.' *American Journal of Orthopsychiatry 59,* 266–278.

Belsky, J. (1980) 'Child maltreatment: an ecological integration.' *American Psychologist 35,* 320–335.

Belsky, J. (1984) 'The determinants of parenting.' *Child Development 55,* 83–96.

Benzeval, M., Judge, K. and Whitehead, M. (1995) *Tackling Inequalities in Health: An Agenda for Action.* London: King's Fund.

Bhugra, D (1996) 'Young homeless and homeless families: a review.' In D. Bhugra (ed) *Homelessness and Mental Health*. Cambridge: Cambridge University Press.

Billingham, K. (1991) 'Public health and the community.' *Health Visitor 64*, 40–43.

Binney, V., Harkell, G. and Nixon, J. (1985) 'Refuges, and housing for battered women.' In J. Pahl (ed) *Private Violence and Public Policy*. London: Routledge.

Blackburn, C. (1991) *Poverty and Health*. Milton Keynes: Open University Press.

Blair, C. and Wrate, R.M. (1997) 'Mental Health.' In R.M. Wrate and P. McLoughlin (eds) *Feeling Bad: The Troubled Lives and Health of Single Young Homeless People in Edinburgh*. Edinburgh: Primary Care Services, Lothian Health.

Blake, J. (1997) 'Exclusion units.' *Roof 22*, 6, 27–28.

Blasi, G. (1990) 'Social policy and social science research on homelessness.' *Journal of Social Issues 46*, 207–219.

Blaxter, M. (1990) Health and Lifestyles. London: Routledge.

Boulton, I. (1993) 'Youth homelessness and health care.' In K. Fisher and J. Collins (eds) *Homelessness, Health Care and Welfare Provision*. London: Routledge.

Bowlby, J. (1980) *Attachment and Loss Vol. 3: Loss, Sadness and Depression*. New York: Basic Books.

Bradburn, H. (1994) *Home Truths: Access to Local Authority and Housing Association Tenancies. Responses to the Consultation Paper*. London: Shelter.

Bronfenbrenner, U. (1979) *The Ecology of Human Development*. Cambridge, MA: Harvard University Press.

Brooks, L. and Patel, M. (1995) *Homelessness and Health: A Right to Health Care, a Challenge for the Health Services*. London: Redbridge and Waltham Forest Health Authority.

Brooks-Gunn, J., Duncan, G.J., Kato, P. and Sealand, N. (1993) 'Do neighbourhoods influence child and adolescent development?' *American Journal of Sociology 99*, 353–395.

Brown, G. and Harris, T. (1978) *The Social Origins of Depression*. London: Tavistock.

Buckner, J.C., Bassuk, E.L. and Zima, B.T. (1993) 'Mental health issues affecting homeless women: implications for intervention.' *American Journal of Orthopsychiatry 63*, 385–399.

Buckner, J.C. and Bassuk, E.L. (1997) 'Mental disorders and service utilization among youths from homeless and low-income housed families.' *Journal of the American Academy of Child and Adolescent Psychiatry 36*, 890–900.

Buckner, J.C., Bassuk, E.L., Weinreb, L.F. and Brooks, M.G. (1999) 'Homelessness and its relation to the mental health and behaviour of low-income school-age children.' *Developmental Psychology*, in press.

Bull, J. (1993) *Housing Consequences of Relationship Breakdown*. London: HMSO.

Bunce, C. (1996) 'A hard road to travel.' *Nursing Times 92*, 34–36.

Calnan, M. (1987) *Health and Illness*. London: Tavistock.

Campbell, R. (1997) 'Mending the safety net.' *Roof 22*, 6, 19.

Caton, C.L.M. (1990) *Homeless in America*. New York: Oxford University Press.

Charles, N. (1993) *The Housing Needs of Women and Children Escaping Domestic Violence.* Cardiff: Tai Cymru.

Charles, N. (1994) 'Domestic violence, homelessness and housing: the response of housing providers in Wales.' *Critical Social Policy 41,* 36–52.

Child Accident Prevention Trust (1991) *Safe as Houses?* London: Child Accident Prevention Trust.

Child Accident Prevention Trust (1992) *Current Practice Guide Number Three.* London: Child Accident Prevention Trust.

Cicchetti, D. and Lynch, M. (1993) 'Toward an ecological/transactional model of community violence and child maltreatment: consequences for children's development.' *Psychiatry 56,* 96–118.

Clapham, D. and Evans, A. (1998) *From Exclusion to Inclusion.* Hastoe Housing Association.

Collard, A. (1997) *Settling up Towards a Strategy for Resettling Homeless Families.* London: London Homeless Forum, Save the Children, Shelter, Health Visitor's Association, National Children's Homes, National Council of Voluntary Child Care Organisations and The Children's Society.

Commander, M., Odell, S. and Sashidharan, S. (1997) 'Psychiatric admission for homeless people: the impact of a specialist community mental health team.' *Psychiatric Bulletin 21,* 260–263.

Committee of Inquiry (1995) *Report of the Inquiry into the Circumstances Leading to the Death of Jonathon Newby.* London: Oxford.

Connelly, J. and Crown, J. (eds) (1994) *Homelessness and Ill Health: Report of a Working Party of the Royal College of Physicians.* London: Royal College of Physicians.

Conway, J. (ed) (1988) *Prescription for Poor Health: the Crisis for Homeless Families.* London: London Food Commission, Maternity Alliance, SHAC and Shelter.

Cooper, P.J. and Goodyer, I. (1993) 'A community study of depression in adolescent girls. I: estimates of symptoms and syndrome prevalence.' *British Journal of Psychiatry 163,* 369–374.

Coulton, C. (1995) 'Using community-level indicators of children's well-being in comprehensive community initiatives.' In J. Connell, A. Kubisch, L. Schorr and C. Weiss (eds) *New Approaches to Evaluating Community Initiatives.* Washington, D.C.: The Aspen Institute.

Cowan, D. (1996) *The Housing Act 1996: A Practical Guide.* Bristol: Jordans.

Craig, T.K.J., Hodson, S., Woodward, S. and Richardson, S. (1996) *Off to a Bad Start: A Longitudinal Study of Homeless Young People in London.* London: The Mental Health Foundation.

Crane, H. (1990) *Speaking from Experience – Working with Homeless Families.* London: Bayswater Hotel Homeless Project.

Cumella, S., Grattan, E. and Vostanis, P. (1998) 'The mental health of children in homeless families, and their contact with health, education, and social services.' *Health and Social Care in the Community 6,* 331–342.

Daly, G. (1989) 'Homelessness and health: views and responses in Canada, the United Kingdom and the United States.' *Health Promotion 4,* 115–127.

Davies, E. (1992) *The Health of Homeless and Hidden Homeless Families in Reading.* Reading: Reading Borough Council and West Berks Health Authority.

Department of the Environment – Department of Health (1996) *Code of Guidance on Parts VI and VII of the Housing Act 1996: Allocation of Housing Accommodation Homelessness.* London: HMSO.

Department for Education and Employment (1997) *Excellence in Schools.* London: HMSO.

Department of Education and Science HMI (1989) *A Study of the Education of Children Living in Temporary Accommodation.* London: HMSO.

Department of Environment (1977) *Housing (Homeless Persons) Act.* London: HMSO.

Department of Environment (1985) *Housing Act.* London: HMSO.

Department of Environment (1989) *The Government's Review of the Homelessness Legislation.* London: HMSO.

Department of Environment (1994) *Access to Local Authority Housing: A Consultation Paper.* London: HMSO.

Department of Environment (1995) *Our Future Homes.* Cmnd 2901, London: HMSO.

Department of Environment (1996) *Housing Act.* London: HMSO.

Department of Health (1989) *Children Act.* London: HMSO.

Department of Health (1992) *The Health of the Nation: A Strategy for Health in England and Wales.* London: HMSO.

Department of Health (1997) *Local Authority Circular: Family Law Act 1996, Part IV. Family Homes and Domestic Violence.* London: Department of Health.

Dobash, R.E. and Dobash, R. (1992) *Women, Violence and Social Change.* London: Routledge.

Drennan, V. and Stern, J. (1986) 'Health visitors and homeless families.' *Health Visitor 59,* 11, 340–342.

Duffield, C. (1993) 'The Delphi technique: a comparison of results obtained using two expert panels.' *International Journal of Nursing Studies 30,* 227 237.

Duncan, G., Brooks-Gunn, J. and Klebanov, P. (1994) 'Economic deprivation and early childhood development.' *Child Development 65,* 296 318.

Earls, F., McGuire, J. and Shay, S. (1994) 'Evaluating a community intervention to reduce the risk of child abuse: methodological strategies in conducting neighbourhood surveys.' *Child Abuse and Neglect 18,* 473 486.

Ellwood, D. (1988) *Poor Support: Poverty in the American Family.* New York: Basic Books.

Eurobarometer (1997) *Eurobarometer 47.2.* Brussels: European Commission DGXXll, 29 July 1997.

Evans, A. (1991) *Alternatives to Bed and Breakfast: Temporary Housing Solutions for Homeless People.* London: National Housing and Town Planning Council.

Evans, A (1996) *We Don't Choose to be Homeless: Report of the National Inquiry into Preventing Youth Homelessness.* London: CHAR (now National Homeless Alliance).

Families in Bayswater Bed and Breakfast (1987) *Speaking for Ourselves*. London: The Bayswater Hotel Homeless Project.

Feitel, B., Margetson, N., Chamas, J. and Lipman, C. (1992) 'Psychosocial background and behavioural and emotional disorder of homeless and runaway youth.' *Hospital and Community Psychiatry 43,* 155 159.

Ferguson, B. and Dixon, R. (1992) 'Psychiatric clinics in homeless hostels your flexible friend.' *Psychiatric Bulletin 16,* 683 684.

Ferran, J., O'Shea, B. and Davidson, I. (1993) 'The homeless and the mental health services: a Liverpool study.' *Psychiatric Bulletin 17,* 649 651.

Fierman, A., Dreyer, B., Quinn, L., Shulman, S., Courtlandt, C. and Guzzo, R. (1991) 'Growth delay in homeless children.' *Pediatrics 88,* 918–925.

Finkelstein, J. and Parker, R. (1993) 'Homeless children in America: taking the next step.' *American Journal of Disease in Childhood 147,* 520–521.

Firth, K. (1995) 'Opening the door to homeless households.' *Health Visitor 68,* 97.

Fischer, P.J. and Breakey, W.R. (1991) 'The epidemiology of alcohol, drug, and mental disorders among homeless persons.' *American Psychologist 46,* 1115–1128.

Fisher, K. and Collins, J. (1993) 'Health care for single homeless people.' In Fisher, K. and Collins, J. (eds) *Homelessness Health Care and Welfare Provision.* London: Routledge.

Fors, S.W. and Jarvis, S. (1995) 'Evaluation of a peer-led drug abuse risk reduction project for runaway/homeless youths.' *Journal of Drug Education 25,* 321–333.

Fox, S., Barrnett, R., Davies, M. and Bird, H. (1990) 'Psychopathology and developmental delay in homeless children: a pilot study.' *Journal of the American Academy of Child and Adolescent Psychiatry 29,* 732–735.

Furstenberg, F. (1993) 'How families manage risk and opportunity in dangerous neighbourhoods.' In W.J. Wilson (ed) *Sociology and the Public Agenda.* Newbury Park, CA: Sage.

Gammon, J. (1996) 'Health services for travelling gypsies: a day in the life of Judith Moreton.' *Auditorium The Anglia and Oxford Journal for Improving Health Care Quality 6,* 12–15.

Garbarino, J. and Kostelny, K. (1992) 'Child abuse as a community problem.' *Child Abuse and Neglect 16,* 455–464.

Garbarino, J. and Kostelny, K. (1995) 'Parenting and public policy.' In M. Bornstein (ed) *Handbook of Parenting, Volume 3, Status and Social Consequences of Parenting.* Mahwah, NJ: Lawrence Erlbaum Associates.

Garcia-Coll, C., Buckner, J.C., Brooks, M.G., Weinreb, L.F. and Bassuk, E.L. (1998) 'The developmental status and adaptive behaviour of homeless and low-income housed infants and toddlers.' *American Journal of Public Health 88,* 1371–1374.

Garfinkel, I. (1992) 'Bringing fathers back in: the child support assurance strategy.' *The American Prospect 9,* 74–83.

Garfinkel, I. (1994) 'The child-support revolution.' American Economic Review 84, 81–85.

Garmezy, D. and Masten, A.S. (1994) 'Chronic adversities.' In M. Rutter, E. Taylor and L. Hersov (eds) Child and Adolescent Psychiatry (3rd edn). Oxford: Blackwell Scientific Publications.

Garmezy, N. and Rutter, M. (eds) (1983) Stress, Coping and Development in Children. New York: McGraw-Hill.

Gewirtz, S., Ball, S. and Bowe, R. (1995) Markets, Choice and Equity in Education. Buckingham: Open University Press.

Gibson, J. (1959) Health, Personal and Communal. London: Faber and Faber.

Gill, B. Meltzer, H., Hinds, K. and Petticrew, M. (1996) Psychiatric Morbidity among Homeless People. OPCS Surveys of Psychiatric Morbidity in Great Britain Report 7. London: HMSO.

Gill, O. (1992) Parenting under Pressure. London: Barnardo's.

Gilroy, R. and Woods, R. (1994) Housing Women. London: Routledge.

Goldberg, D. and Hillier, V. (1979) 'A scaled version of the General Health Questionnaire.' Psychological Medicine 9, 139–145.

Goldberg, D. and Huxley, P. (1980) Mental Illness in the Community: The Pathways to Psychiatric Care. London: Tavistock.

Goldberg, D. and Huxley, P. (1992) Common Mental Disorders: A Bio-Social Model. London: Tavistock/Routledge.

Goldberg, D., Rickels, K., Downing, R. and Hesbacher, P. (1976) 'A comparison of two psychiatric screening tests.' British Journal of Psychiatry 129, 61–67.

Goodman, R. (1997) 'Child mental health: an overextended remit.' British Medical Journal 314, 813–814.

Goodman, L.A. (1991a) 'The prevalence of abuse among homeless and housed poor mothers: a comparison study.' American Journal of Orthopsychiatry 61, 489–500.

Goodman, L.A. (1991b) 'The relationship between social support and family homelessness: a comparison study of homeless and housed mothers.' Journal of Community Psychology 19, 321–332.

Goodwin, J. and Grant, C. (1997) (eds) Built to Last. London: ROOF Magazine.

Goodyer, I. (1990) Life Experiences, Development and Childhood Psychopathology. Chichester: Wiley.

Goodyer, I., Wright, C. and Altham, P. (1989) 'Recent friendships in anxious and depressed school-age children.' Psychological Medicine 19, 165–174.

Grace, S. (1995) Policing Domestic Violence in the 1990s. Home Office Research Study 139. London: Home Office.

Graham, H. (1993) 'Women's smoking: government targets and social trends.' Health Visitor 66, 80–82.

Greene, J.M., Ennett, S.T. and Ringwalt, C.L. (1997) 'Substance use among runaway and homeless youth in three national samples.' American Journal of Public Health 87, 229–235.

Gregory, S. (1998) Transforming Local Services: Partnership in Action. York: Joseph Rowntree Foundation.

Greve, J. (1991) Homelessness in Britain. York: Joseph Rowntree Foundation.

Griffiths, M., Parker, J., Smith, R., Stirling, T. and Trott, T. (1996) *Community Lettings: Local Allocation Policies in Practice.* York: Joseph Rowntree Foundation.

Griffiths, M., Parker, J., Smith, R. and Stirling, T. (1997) *Local Authority Housing Allocations: Systems, Policies and Procedures.* London: Department of the Environment, Transport and the Regions.

Griffiths-Jones, A. (1997) 'Tuberculosis in homeless people.' *Nursing Times 93,* 60–61.

Gruber, A.J., Pope, H.G. and Brown, M.E. (1996) 'Do patients use marijuana as an antidepressant?' *Depression 4,* 77–80.

Hague, G. (1997) 'Smoke screen or leap forward: inter-agency initiatives as a response to domestic violence.' *Critical Social Policy 17,* 93–109.

Hague, G., Kelly, L., Malos, E. and Mullender, A. (1996) *Children, Domestic Violence and Refuges.* Bristol: WAFE.

Hague G. and Malos E. (1993, new edition 1998) *Domestic Violence: Action for Change.* Cheltenham: New Clarion Press.

Hague, G. and Malos, E. (1994a) 'Children, domestic violence and housing: the impact of homelessness.' In A. Mullender and R. Morley (eds) *Children Living with Domestic Violence.* London: Whiting and Birch.

Hague, G. and Malos, E. (1994b) 'Domestic violence, social policy and housing.' *Critical Social Policy 42,* 112–125.

Hague, G., Malos, E. and Dear, W. (1996) *Multi-Agency Work and Domestic Violence: A National Study of Inter-Agency Initiatives.* Bristol: Policy Press.

Hammond, L. and Bell, J. (1995) 'The setting up of a drop-in service to a homeless families project: systemic issues and clinical implications.' *Newsletter of the Association of Child Psychology and Psychiatry 17,* 132–138.

Harwin, N., Malos, E. and Hague, G. (1998 forthcoming) *Domestic Violence and Multi-Agency Working: New Opportunities, Old Challenges?* London: Whiting and Birch.

Hausman, B. and Hammen, C. (1993) 'Parenting in homeless families: the double crisis.' *American Journal of Orthopsychiatry 63,* 358–369.

Health Visitors' Association and General Medical Services Council (1989) *Homeless Families and their Health.* London: British Medical Association.

Heath, I. (1994) 'The poor man at his gate: homelessness is an avoidable cause of ill health.' *British Medical Journal 309,* 1675–1676.

Henderson S., Byrne D. and Duncan-Jones, P. (1981) *Neurosis and the Social Environment.* Australia: Academic Press.

Her Majesty's Inspectorate of Schools (1990) *A Survey of the Education of Children Living in Temporary Accommodation, April–December 1989.* London: Department of Education and Science.

Herman, D., Susser, E., Struening, E. and Link, B. (1997) 'Adverse childhood experiences: are they risk factors for adult homelessness?' *American Journal of Public Health 87,* 249–255.

HMSO (1985) *Physical and Social Survey of Houses in Multiple Occupation in England and Wales.* London: HMSO.

HMSO (1994) *The Criminal Justice and Public Order Act.* London: HMSO.

HMSO (1996) *The Asylum and Immigration Act.* London: HMSO.

HMSO (1996) *Family Law Act.* London: HMSO.

HMSO (1997) *Prevention of Harassment Act.* London: HMSO.

Hodnicki, D. and Horner, S. (1993) 'Homeless mothers caring for children in a shelter.' *Issues in Mental Health Nursing 14,* 349–356.

Hoffbauer, D. and Prenn, M. (1996) 'A place to call one's own: choosing books about homelessness.' *Social Education 60,* 167–169.

Holmes, C. (1998) 'Is it asking too much?' *Roof 23,* 2, 10–11.

Home Office (1995) *Inter-Agency Circular: Inter-Agency Coordination to Tackle Domestic Violence.* London: Home Office.

Home Office (1990) *Circular 60/90.* London: Home Office.

Housing (Homeless Persons) Act (1977). London: HMSO.

Hu, D., Covell, R., Morgan, J. and Arcia, J. (1989) 'Health care needs for children of the recently homeless.' *Journal of Community Health 14,* 1–8.

Hutchinson, K. (1992) *Specialist Health Visitor for Homeless Families.* Reading: Priority Care Service, unpublished report.

Hutchinson, K. (1994) *Specialist Health Visitor for Homeless Families.* Reading: Priority Care Service, unpublished report.

Hutchinson, K. (1996) *Report on the South Reading Stair Gate Scheme.* Reading: Priority Care Service, unpublished report.

Hutchinson, K. (1997) *A Study to Determine the Health Priorities of Homeless Families and how they Compare to Health Visiting Priorities.* Reading: University of Reading, unpublished MA dissertation.

Hutchinson, K. and Gutteridge, B. (1995) 'Health visiting homeless families: the role of the specialist health visitor.' *Health Visitor 69,* 372–374.

Huttenmoser, M. (1995) 'Children and their living surroundings: empirical investigations into the significance of living surroundings for the everyday life and development of children.' *Children's Environments 12,* 403–414.

Inner London Education Authority (1987) *Homeless Families: Implications for Educational Provision.* London: ILEA.

Irvine, M. (1996) *The Housing Act 1996: A Guide.* Coventry: Chartered Institute of Housing.

Janus, M.D., Archambault, F.X., Brown, S.W. and Welsh, L.A. (1995) 'Physical abuse in Canadian runaway adolescents.' *Child Abuse and Neglect 19,* 433–447.

Jencks, C. (1992) *Rethinking Social Policy: Race, Poverty and the Underclass.* Cambridge, MA: Harvard University Press.

Jezewski, M.A. (1995) 'Staying connected: the core of facilitating health care for homeless persons.' *Public Health Nursing 12,* 203–210.

Jones G. (1995) *Leaving Home.* Buckingham: Open University Press.

Joseph Rowntree Foundation (1996) *The Future of the Voluntary Sector. Social Policy Summary 9.* York: Joseph Rowntree Publications.

Karmi, G. (1993) 'Equity and health of ethnic minorities.' *Quality in Health Care 2*, 100–103.

Kessler, R.C., McGonagle, K.A., Zhao, S., Nelson, C.B. and Hughes, M. (1994) 'Lifetime and 12-month prevalence of DSM-III-R psychiatric disorders in the United States.' *Archives of General Psychiatry 51*, 8–19.

Kingdom, K.H. (1960) 'Relative humidity and air-borne infections.' *American Review of Respiratory Disease 81*, 504–512.

Koegel, P., Burnam, M.A. and Baumohl, J. (1996) 'The causes of homelessness.' In J. Baumohl (ed) *Homelessness in America*. Phoenix, AZ: Oryx Press.

Koegel, P., Melamid, E. and Burnam A. (1995) 'Childhood risk factors for homelessness among homeless adults.' *American Journal of Public Health 85*, 1642–1649.

Kovacs, M. (1996) 'Presentation and course of major depressive disorder during childhood and later years of the life span.' *Journal of the American Academy of Child and Adolescent Psychiatry 35*, 705–715.

Kozol, J. (1988) *Rachel and her Children: Homeless Families in America*. New York: Crown.

Kral, A.H., Molnar, B.E., Booth, R.E. and Watters, J.K. (1997) 'Prevalence of sexual risk behaviour and substance use among runaway and homeless adolescents in San Francisco, Denver and New York.' *International Journal of STD and AIDS 8*, 109–117.

Kurtz, Z., Thornes, R. and Wolkind, S. (1994) *Services for the Mental Health of Children and Young People in England: A National Review*. London: South Thames Regional Health Authority.

Labour Party (1995) *Peace at Home*. London: Labour Party.

Lewis, G., Pelosi, A.J., Araya, R.C. and Dunn, G. (1992) 'Measuring psychiatric disorder in the community: a standardized assessment for use by lay interviewers.' *Psychological Medicine 22*, 465–486.

Lissauer, T., Richman, S., Tempia, M., Jenkins, S. and Taylor, B. (1993) 'Influence of homelessness on acute admissions to hospital.' *Archives of Disease in Childhood 69*, 423–429.

London Research Centre (1998) 'LRC update: homelessness.' *Roof 23*, 1.

Loosley, S. (1994) 'Women's Community House Children's Program.' In A. Mullender and R. Morley (eds) *Children Living with Domestic Violence*. London: Whiting and Birch.

Lovell, B. (1986) 'Health visiting homeless families.' *Health Visitor 59*, 11, 334–337.

McCann, J.M., James, A., Wilson, S. and Dunn, G. (1996) 'Prevalence of psychiatric disorders in young people in the care system.' *British Medical Journal 313*, 1529–1530.

McMillan, D. and Chavis, D. (1986) 'Sense of community: a definition and theory.' *Journal of Community Psychology 14*, 6–23.

Malos E. (1993) *You've Got No Life*. Bristol: School of Applied Social Studies, University of Bristol.

Malos, E. and Hague G. (1993) *Domestic Violence and Housing.* Bristol: WAFE and School of Applied Social Studies, University of Bristol.

Malos, E. and Hague, G. (1997) 'Women, housing and homelessness, and domestic violence.' *Women's Studies International Forum 20,* 397–409.

Malos, E. and Hague G. (1998) 'Facing both ways at once: the effect of the Housing Act 1996 on legislations and policy for women and children escaping domestic violence.' In D. Cowan (ed) *Housing: Participation and Exclusion.* Devon: Dartmouth Publishing.

Mama, A. (1996) *The Hidden Struggle: Statutory and Voluntary Sector Responses to Violence against Black Women in the Home.* London: Whiting and Birch.

Marshall, M. (1996) 'The severely mentally ill in hostels for the homeless'. In D. Bhugra (ed) Homelessness and Mental Health.

Masten, A.S., Miliotis, D., Graham-Berman, S.A., Ramirez, M. and Neemann, J. (1993) 'Children in homeless families: risks to mental health and development.' *Journal of Consulting and Clinical Psychology 61,* 335–343.

Maxwell, R.J. (1984). 'Quality Assessment in health.' *British Medical Journal 288,* 1470–1473.

Means, R. (1997) 'From the Poor Law to the marketplace'. In J. Goodwin and C. Grant (eds) *Built to Last?* Second edition, London: ROOF magazine.

Milburn, N. and D'Ercole, A. (1991) 'Homeless women. moving towards a comprehensive model.' *American Psychologist 46,* 1161–1169.

Miller, D. and Lin, E. (1988) 'Children in sheltered homeless families: reported health status and use of health services.' *Pediatrics 81,* 668–673.

Miller, M. (1990) *Bed-and-Breakfast: a Study of Women and Homelessness Today.* London: Women's Press.

Mirrlees-Black, C. (1995) 'Estimating the extent of domestic violence.' *Research Bulletin 37,* 1–9.

Molnar, J. and Rath, W. (1990) 'Constantly compromised: the impact of homelessness in children.' *Journal of Social Issues 46,* 109–124.

Molnar, J., Rath, W.R., Klein, T.P., Lowe, C. and Hartmann, A.H. (1991) *Ill Fares in the Land: The Consequences of Homelessness and Chronic Poverty for Children and Families in New York City.* New York: Bank Street College of Education.

Montgomery, C. (1994) 'Swimming upstream: the strengths of women who survive homelessness.' *Advances in Nursing Science 16,* 34–45.

Mooney, J. (1994) *Researching Domestic Violence: The North London Domestic Violence Survey.* London: London Borough of Islington.

Morton, E. (1997) *South Yorkshire Multi-Agency Monitoring of Young People in Housing Need.* London: Shelter.

Muir, J. and Ross M. (1993) *Housing and the Poorer Sex.* London: London Housing Unit.

Mullender, A. (1996) *Rethinking Domestic Violence: The Social Work and Probation Response.* London: Routledge.

Mullender, A. and Morley, R. (1994) *Children Living with Domestic Violence.* London: Whiting and Birch.

Mullins, D. and Niner, P. (1996) *Evaluation of the 1991 Homelessness Code of Guidance.* London: HMSO.

Mundy, P., Robertson, M., Robertson, J. and Greenblatt, M. (1990) 'The prevalence of psychotic symptoms in homeless adolescents.' *Journal of the American Academy of Child and Adolescent Psychiatry 29,* 724–731.

National Research Council Panel on Research on Child Abuse and Neglect (1993) *Understanding Child Abuse and Neglect.* Washington, DC: National Academy Press.

National Assistance Act (1948). London: HMSO.

National Consumer Council (1992) *Death Trap Housing.* London: National Consumer Council.

National Children's Homes Action for Children (1996) *Fact File 96 / 97.* London: NCH Action for Children.

Newson, J. and Newson, E. (1965) *Patterns of Infant Care in an Urban Community.* Harmondsworth: Penguin.

Niner, P. (1989) *Homelessness in Nine Local Authorities: Case Studies of Policy and Practice.* London: HMSO.

Niner, P. (1997) *The Early Impact of the Housing Act 1996 and Housing Benefit Changes.* London: Shelter.

North, C., Thompson, S., Smith, E. and Kyburz, L. (1996) 'Violence in the lives of homeless mothers in a substance abuse treatment programme: a descriptive study.' *Journal of Interpersonal Violence 11,* 234–249.

O'Callaghan, B. and Dominian, L. (1996) *A Study of Homeless Applicants.* London: HMSO, Department of the Environment.

Office of Population Censuses and Surveys (1980) *Classification of Occupations 1980.* London: HMSO.

Office of Population Censuses and Surveys (1992) *General Household Survey 1990.* London: HMSO.

Olds, D.L., Henderson, CR., Chamberlain, R. and Tatelbaum, R. (1986) 'Preventing child abuse and neglect: a randomized trial of nurse home visitation.' *Pediatrics 78,* 65–78.

Oppenheim, C. and Harker, L. (1996) *Poverty: the Facts (3rd edn).* London: Child Poverty Action Group.

Parker, R., Rescorla, L., Finkelstein, J., Barnes, N., Holmes, J. and Stolley, P. (1991) 'A survey of the health of homeless children in Philadelphia shelters.' *American Journal of Disease in Childhood 145,* 520–526.

Parliamentary Select Committee on Violence in Marriage (1975) *Report from the Select Committee on Violence in Marriage.* London: HMSO.

Parsons, L. (1991) 'Homeless families in Hackney.' *Public Health 105,* 287–296.

Patterson, C. and Roderick, P. (1990) 'Obstetric outcome in homeless women.' *British Medical Journal 301,* 263–266.

Patton, M. (1996) 'Where do you live when you don't have a house?' *Social Studies and the Young Learner 8,* 14–16.

Pearce, J. (1993) 'Child health surveillance for psychiatric disorders: practical guidelines.' *Archives of Disease in Childhood 69,* 394–398.

Pence, E. (1988) *Batterers' Programs: Shifting from Community Collusion to Community Confrontation.* Duluth, Minnesota: Duluth Domestic Abuse Intervention Project.

Peterman, P.J. (1981) 'Parenting and environmental considerations.' *American Journal of Orthopsychiatry 5,* 351–355.

Platt, S.P., Martin, C.J. and Hunt, S.M. (1989) 'Damp housing, mould growth and symptomatic health state.' *British Medical Journal 298,* 1673–1678.

Pleace, N. and Quilgars, D. (1996) *Health and Homelessness in London.* London: King's Fund.

Pound, A. and Mills, M. (1985) 'A pilot evaluation of Newpin-home visiting and befriending scheme in south London.' *Newsletter of the Association of Child Psychology and Psychiatry 7,* 13–15.

Power, A. and Tunstall, R. (1995) *Swimming Against the Tide: Progress and Polarisation on Twenty Unpopular Council Estates 1980–95.* York: Joseph Rowntree Foundation.

Power, S., Whitty, G. and Youdell, D. (1995) *No Place to Learn: Homelessness and Education.* London: Shelter.

Prime, D. (1997) *Crawley and Horsham Multi-Agency Monitoring of Young People in Housing Need.* London: Shelter.

Puddifoot, J. (1996) 'Some initial considerations in the measurement of community identity.' *Journal of Community Psychology 24,* 327–336.

Quinton, D and Rutter, M. (1984) 'Parenting behaviour of mothers raised in care.' In A.R. Nicol (ed) *Longitudinal Studies in Child Psychology and Psychiatry.* Chichester: Wiley.

Rafferty, Y. (1991) 'Developmental and educational consequences of homelessness on children and youth.' In J. Kryder-Coe, L. Salamon and J. Molnar (eds) *Homeless Children and Youth: A New American Dilemma.* New Brunswick, Canada: Transaction Publications.

Rafferty, Y. and Shinn, M. (1991) 'The impact of homelessness on children.' *American Psychologist 46,* 1170–1179.

Rainwater, L. (1966) 'Fear and the house-as-haven in the lower class.' *Journal of the American Institute of Planners 32,* 23–31.

Raychaba, B. (1989) 'Canadian youth in care: leaving care to be on our own with no direction from home.' *Children and Youth Services Review 11,* 61–73.

Reimer, J.G., Van Cleve, L. and Galbraith, M. (1995) 'Barriers to well child care for homeless children under age 13.' *Public Health Nursing 12,* 61–66.

Rescorla, L., Parker, R. and Stolley, P. (1991) 'Ability, achievement, and adjustment in homeless children.' *American Journal of Orthopsychiatry 61,* 2, 210–220.

Resource Information Service (1996) *Emergency Hostels: Direct Access Accommodation in London.* London: Resource Information Service.

Richman, N., Stevenson, J. and Graham, P. (1982) *Pre-School to School: A Behavioural Study.* London: Academic Press.

Richman, S., Roderick, P., Victor, C.R. and Lissauer, T. (1991) 'The use of acute hospital services by homeless children.' *Public Health 105,* 297–302.

Richters, J. and Martinez, P.E. (1993) 'Violent communities, family choices, and children's chances: an algorithm for improving the odds.' *Development and Psychopathology 5,* 609–627.

Robertson, C. (1991) *Health Visiting in Practice (2nd edn).* London: Churchill Livingstone.

Robins, L. (1970) 'Follow-up studies investigating childhood disorders.' In E. Hare and J. Wing (eds) *Psychiatric Epidemiology.* Oxford: Oxford University Press.

Robins, L. (1978) 'Study of childhood predictors of adult anti-social behaviour.' *Psychological Medicine 8,* 611–622.

Rog, D., McCombs-Thornton, K., Gilbert-Mongelli, A., Brito, M.C. and Holupka C.S. (1995) 'Implementation of the homeless families program: 2. Characteristics, strengths and needs of participating families.' *American Journal of Orthopsychiatry 65,* 514–528.

Rossi, P.H. (1989) *Down and Out in America: the Origins of Homelessness.* Chicago: University of Chicago Press.

Rossi, P.H. (1994) 'Troubling families: family homelessness in America.' *American Behavioral Scientist 37,* 342–395.

Rotheram-Borus, M.J., Mahler, K.A., Koopman, C. and Langabeer, K. (1996) 'Sexual abuse history and associated multiple risk behaviour in adolescent runaways.' *American Journal of Orthopsychiatry 66,* 390–400.

Royal College of Physicians Working Party (1994) *Homelessness and Ill Health.* London: Royal College of Physicians.

Rubin, D.H., Erickson, C.J., Agustin, M.S., Cleary, S.D. Allen, J.K. and Cohen, P. (1996) 'Cognitive and academic functioning of homeless children compared with housed children.' *Pediatrics 93,* 89–294.

Rutter, M. (1966) *Children of Sick Parents: An Environmental and Psychiatric Study.* London: Oxford University Press.

Rutter, M. (1981). 'Stress, coping and development: some issues and some perspectives.' *Journal of Child Psychology and Psychiatry 22,* 323–356.

Rutter, M. (1984) 'Family and school influences.' In A.R. Nicol (ed) *Longitudinal Studies in Child Psychology and Psychiatry.* Chichester: Wiley.

Rutter, M. (1985) 'Resilience in the face of adversity: protective factors and resistance to psychiatric disorder.' *British Journal of Psychiatry 147,* 598–611.

Rutter, M. and Quinton, D. (1984) 'Parental psychiatric disorder: effects on children.' *Psychological Medicine 14,* 853–880.

Rutter, M. and Smith, D.J. (eds) (1990) *Psychosocial Disorders in Young People: Time Trends and their Causes.* Chichester: J Wiley & Sons.

Sampson, R.J. (1992) 'Family management and child development: insights from social disorganization theory.' In J. McCord (ed) *Advances in Criminological Theory, Volume 3.* New Brunswick, NJ: Transaction.

Sampson, R.J. and Groves, W. (1989). 'Community structure and crime: testing social-disorganization theory.' *American Journal of Sociology 94*, 774–802.

Scanlon, T., Tomkins, A., Lynch, M. and Scanlon, F. (1998) 'Street children in Latin America.' *British Medical Journal 316*, 1596–1600.

Schteingart, J., Molnar, J., Klein, T., Lowe, C. and Hartmann, A. (1995) 'Homelessness and child functioning in the context of risk and protective factors moderating child outcomes.' *Journal of Clinical Child Psychology 24*, 320–331.

Sclar, E.D. (1990) 'Homelessness and housing policy: a game of musical chairs (editorial).' *American Journal of Public Health 80*, 1039–1040.

Scott, J. (1993) 'Homelessness and mental illness.' *British Journal of Psychiatry 162*, 314–324.

Sebba, R. and Churchman, A. (1986) 'The uniqueness of the home.' *Architecture and Behaviour 3*, 7–24.

Seedhouse, M. (1986) *Health: the Foundation for Achievement.* Chichester: John Wiley and Sons.

Shaffer, D. and Caton, C.L.M. (1984) *Runaway and Homeless Youth in New York City.* New York: Ittleston Foundation.

Shaffer, D., Fisher, P., Dulcan, M.K., Davies, M., Piacentini, J., Schwab-Stone, M., Lahey, B., Bourdon, K., Jensen, P., Bird, H., Canino, G. and Regier, D. (1996) 'The NIMH Diagnostic Interview Schedule for Children Version 2.3 (DISC-2.3): description, acceptability, prevalence rates, and performance in the MECA Study.' *Journal of the American Academy of Child and Adolescent Psychiatry 35*, 865–877.

Sharma, R. (1987) *No Place like Home: A Report by the West London Homeless Group.* London: West London Homelessness Group.

Shelter (1994) *Action.* London: Shelter Policy Unit.

Shelter Policy Unit (1997) *Shelter Briefing, Parts VI and VII Housing Act 199.* London: Shelter Policy Unit.

Shinn, M. (1997) 'Family homelessness: state or trait?' *American Journal of Community Psychology 25*, 755–769.

Shinn, M., Knickman, J.R. and Weitzman, B.C. (1991) 'Social relationships and vulnerability to becoming homeless among poor families.' *American Psychologist 46*, 1180–1187.

Simcha-Fagan, O. and Schwartz, J. (1986) 'Neighbourhood and delinquency: an assessment of contextual effects.' *Criminology 24*, 667–703.

Smith, E. and North, C. (1994) 'Not all homeless women are alike: effects of motherhood and the presence of children.' *Community Mental Health Journal 30*, 601–610.

Social Services Inspectorate (1997) *When Leaving Home is also Leaving Care: An Inspection of Services for Young People Leaving Care.* London: Department of Health.

Sparrow S., Bella D. and Cichetti D. (1984) *Vineland Adaptive Behaviour Scales.* Circle Pines, USA: American Guidance Services.

Spencer, N. (1993) 'Commentary.' *Archives of Disease in Childhood 69*, 428–429.

Stanko, E., Crisp, D., Hale, C. and Lucraft, H. (1998) *Counting the Costs: Estimating the Impact of Domestic Violence in the London Borough of Hackney.* London: Crime Concern.

Stearn, J. (1986) 'An expensive way of making children ill.' *Roof 9,* 10, 11–14.

Stepien, D., Lawrence, B., Murray, L. and Clark, A. (1996) *Homelessness, Schooling and Attainment: An Interim Report.* Portsmouth: University of Portsmouth.

Stewart, G. and Stewart, J. (1992) 'Social work with homeless families.' *British Journal of Social Work 22,* 271–289.

Stitt S., Griffiths, G. and Grant, D. (1994) 'Homeless and hungry: the evidence from Liverpool.' *Nutrition and Health 9,* 275–287.

Stone, I. (1997) *Lincolnshire Multi-Agency Monitoring of Young People in Housing Need.* London: Shelter.

Stronge, J.H. (1992) 'The background: history and problems of schooling for the homeless.' In J.H. Stronge (ed) *Educating Homeless Children and Adolescents: Evaluating Policy and Practice.* Newbury Park, USA: Sage Publications.

Tanner, J. and Whitehouse, R. (1975) *Growth and Development Record.* London: Castlemead Publications.

Thomas, A. and Niner, P. (1989) *Living in Temporary Accommodation: A Survey of Homeless People in London.* London: HMSO.

Thomas, A., Chess, S. and Birch, H. (1968) *Temperament and Behaviour Disorders in Children.* London: University of London Press.

Thomas, A. and Hedges, A. (1986) *The 1985 Physical and Social Survey of Houses of Multiple Occupation in England and Wales.* London: Department of the Environment, HMSO.

Thompson, M., Stevenson, J., Sonuga-Barke, E., Nott, P., Bhatti, Z., Price, A. and Hudswell, M. (1995) 'Mental health of preschool children and their mothers in a mixed urban/rural population: I. Prevalence and ecological factors.' *British Journal of Psychiatry 168,* 16–20.

Timms, P. and Balazs, J. (1997) 'Mental health on the margins.' *British Medical Journal 315,* 536–539.

Tomas, A. and Dittmar, H. (1995) 'Housing histories and the meaning of home'. *Housing Studies 10,* 493–515.

Townsend, P. and Davidson, N. (eds) (1982) *Inequalities in Health.* London: Penguin.

Tunstill, J. and Aldgate, J. (1994) *Implementing Section 17 of the Children Act: the First 18 Months: a Study for the Department of Health.* Leicester: Leicester University.

Twaite, J. and Lampert, D.T. (1997) 'Outcomes of mandated preventive services programs for homeless and truant children: a follow-up study.' *Social Work 42,* 11–18.

United Nations (1995) *Platform for Action.* New York: United Nations.

US Bureau of the Census (1996) *Money Income in the United States: 1995. Current Population Reports, P60 193.* Washington, DC: US Government Printing Office.

US Conference of Mayors (1996) *A Status Report of Hunger and Homelessness in America's Cities: 1996.* Washington, DC: Author.

US Department of Housing and Urban Development (1989) *A Report on the 1988 National Survey of Shelters for the Homeless*. Washington, DC: Author.

Usherwood, T., Jones, N. and Hanover Project Team (1993) 'Self-perceived health status of hostel residents: use of the SF-36D health survey questionnaire.' *Journal of Public Health Medicine 15,* 311–314.

Vickers, M. (1991) *Health and Living Conditions of Homeless Families in Oxford City: Literature Review and Analysis of Collected Data.* Unpublished report, Oxford District Health Authority Community Unit/Oxford City Council Environmental Health Department.

Vickers, M. (1991) *Health and Living Conditions of Homeless Families in Oxford City.* Oxford: Oxford District Health Authority, Environmental Health Department.

Victor, C.R. (1992) 'Health status of the temporarily homeless population and residents on North West Thames Region.' *British Medical Journal 305,* 387–392.

Victor, C.R. (1996) 'The health of the temporary homeless population.' *Journal of Interprofessional Care 10,* 3, 257–266.

Victor, C.R. (1997) 'Health of homeless people in Britain: a review.' *European Journal of Public Health 7,* 4, 398–404.

Victor, C.R., Connelly, J., Roderick, P. and Cohen, C. (1989) 'Use of hospital services by homeless families in an inner London health district.' *British Medical Journal 299,* 725–727.

Victor, C.R., Jefferies, S. and Barrett, E. (1990) *The Evaluation of the Bayswater Families Care Team, Research Report 7.* Unpublished report, Parkside Health Authority, Department of Public Health.

Vostanis, P., Cumella, S., Briscoe, J. and Oyebode, F. (1996) 'A survey of psychosocial characteristics of homeless families.' *European Journal of Psychiatry 10,* 108–117.

Vostanis, P., Grattan, E. and Cumella, S. (1998) 'Mental health problems of homeless children and families: a longitudinal study.' *British Medical Journal 316,* 899 902.

Vostanis, P., Grattan, E., Cumella, S. and Winchester, C. (1997) 'Psychosocial functioning of homeless children.' *Journal of the American Academy of Child and Adolescent Psychiatry 36,* 881–889.

Wachs, T.D. and Camli, O. (1991) 'Do ecological or individual characteristics mediate the influence of the physical environment upon maternal behaviour?' *Journal of Environmental Psychology 11,* 249–264.

Weinreb, L.F. and Buckner, J.C. (1993) 'Homeless families: programme responses and public policies.' *American Journal of Orthopsychiatry 63,* 400–409.

Weinreb, L.F., Goldberg, R. and Perloff, J.N. (1998) 'The health characteristics and service use patterns of sheltered homeless and low-income housed mothers.' *Journal of General Internal Medicine 13,* 389–397.

Weinreb, L.F. and Rossi, P. (1995) 'The American homeless family shelter "system".' *Social Service Review 69,* 86–107.

Weitzman, B.C., Knickman, J.R. and Shinn, M. (1992) 'Predictors of shelter use among low-income families: psychiatric history, substance abuse, and victimization.' *American Journal of Public Health 82,* 1547–1550.

Welsh Women's Aid (1994) *Welsh Women's Aid Response to Government Green Paper: Access to Local Authority and Housing Association Tenancies.* Cardiff: Welsh Women's Aid.

Werner, E. (1996) 'Vulnerable but invincible: high risk children from birth to adulthood.' *European Child and Adolescent Psychiatry 5* (Supplement 1), 47–51.

West, P. and Sweeting, H. (1996) 'Nae job, nae future: young people and health in a context of unemployment.' *Health and Social Care in the Community 4,* 50–62.

West, T. (1997) 'Counted out.' *Housing Today 57,* 12–13.

Whitbeck, L.B., Hoyt, D.R. and Ackley, K.A. (1997) 'Families of homeless and runaway adolescents: a comparison of parent/caretaker and adolescent perspectives on parenting, family violence, and adolescent conduct.' *Child Abuse and Neglect 21,* 517–528.

Whitty, G., Power, S. and Halpin, D. (1998) *Devolution and Choice in Education: The School, the State and the Market.* Buckingham: Open University Press.

Whynes, D.K. and Giggs, J.A. (1992) 'The health of the Nottingham homeless'. *Public Health 106,* 307–314.

Wiggans, A. (1989) 'Youth work and homelessness in England.' *Children and Youth Services Review 11,* 5–29.

Wilcox, S. (1997) *Housing Finance Review 1997/98.* London: Joseph Rowntree Foundation.

Williams, P.L. and Webb, C.W. (1994) 'The Delphi technique: a methodological discussion.' *Journal of Advanced Nursing 19,* 180–186.

Williams, R. and Avebury, K. (eds) (1995) *A Place in Mind. Commissioning and Providing Mental Health Services for People who are Homeless.* London: HMSO.

Williams, R. and Richardson, G. (eds)(1995) *Together We Stand: The Commissioning, Role and Management of Child and Adolescent Mental Health Services.* London: HMSO.

Willmot, P. (1986) *Social Networks, Informal Care and Public Policy.* London: Policy Studies Institute.

Wilson, W.J. (1987) *The Truly Disadvantaged: The Inner City, the Underclass, and Public Policy.* Chicago: The University of Chicago Press.

Windle, R.C. and Windle, M. (1997) 'An investigation of adolescents' substance use behaviours, depressed affect, and suicidal behaviours.' *Journal of Child Psychology and Psychiatry 38,* 921–930.

Women's Aid Federation of England (1994) *WAFE Response to the DoE Consultation Paper: Access to Local Authority and Housing Association Tenancies.* Bristol: WAFE.

Wood, D., Valdez, R.B., Hayashi, T. and Shen, A. (1990a) 'Homeless and housed families in Los Angeles: a study comparing demographic, economic and family function characteristics.' *American Journal of Public Health 80,* 1049–1052.

Wood, D., Valdez, R., Hayashi, T. and Shen, A. (1990b) 'Health of homeless children and housed, poor children.' *Pediatrics 86,* 858–866.

Wrate, R.M. (1997) 'General physical health.' In R.M. Wrate and P. McLoughlin (eds) *Feeling Bad: The Troubled Lives and Health of Single Young Homeless People in Edinburgh.* Edinburgh: Primary Care Services, Lothian Health.

Wrate, R.M., Harris, N., Scott, J. and Currie, P. (1997) 'Social contacts and lifestyle indicators.' In R.M. Wrate and P. McLoughlin (eds) *Feeling Bad: The Troubled Lives and Health of Single Young Homeless People in Edinburgh.* Edinburgh: Primary Care Services, Lothian Health.

Wrate, R.M. and McLoughlin, P. (eds) (1997) *Feeling Bad: The Troubled Lives and Health of Single Young Homeless People in Edinburgh.* Edinburgh: Primary Care Services, Lothian Health.

Young, M. and Willmot, P. (1957) *Family and Kinship in East London.* London: Routledge and Kegan Paul.

Ziesemer, C., Marcoux, L. and Marwell, B. (1994) 'Homeless children: are they different from other low-income children?' *Social Work 39,* 658–668.

Zima, B.T., Wells, K.B., Benjamin, B. and Duan, N. (1996) 'Mental health problems among homeless mothers: relationship to service use and child mental health problems.' *Archives of General Psychiatry 53,* 332–338.

Zima, B.T., Wells, K.B. and Freeman, H.E. (1994) 'Emotional and behavioural problems and severe academic delays among sheltered homeless children in Los Angeles County.' *American Journal of Public Health 84,* 260–264.

Zuravin, S.J. and Taylor, R. (1987) 'The ecology of child maltreatment: identifying and characterizing high-risk neighbourhoods.' *Child Welfare 66,* 497–506.

Index